101 Home Based Businesses for Pet Lovers

101 Home Based Businesses for Pet Lovers

Louise Louis

Canyon New Media LLC
Las Vegas

Copyright © 2004 Canyon New Media, LLC

All rights reserved. No part of this book may be reproduced or transmitted in any form or by an electronic or mechanical means including information storage and retrieval systems without permission in writing from the publisher, except by a reviewer, who may quote brief passages in a review.

Library of Congress Control Number: 2003097312
ISBN: 1-879872-00-5
Printed in the United States of America
Canyon New Media, LLC
6900 Westcliff #801
Las Vegas, NV 89145-0617

This publication is designed to provide information to assist individuals in starting a pet related business at home. It is sold with the understanding that the publisher and the author are not engaged to render legal, accounting, or other professional services. If legal advice or other expert assistance is required, the services of a competent professional should be sought.

Companies and associations mentioned by the publisher and author in this book are not being recommended. Their names are provided as a service to readers, and it is up to readers to investigate any company or association.

Readers are encouraged to contact the publisher, Canyon New Media, LLC. or the author, `louise@toybreeds.com` with comments, identification of any broken hyperlinks or suggestions for future editions.

If you enjoy this book, please leave a review of it at your favorite online bookstore such as `www.amazon.com` or `www.bn.com`.

Table of Contents

Before You Start Your Business 5
    Can You Work With the Animals? 7
    Three Places To Visit Before Starting Your Business 10
    Quick and Easy Way to Keep the Books 12
    Four Marketing Methods You Should Avoid 16
    Nine Marketing Methods You Should Use 19
    Care and Feeding of Clients and Customers 24
    Four Most Trying Legal Issues 29
    Four Ethical Concerns 33
    Resources Every Pet Business Should Know 36
101 Home-Based Businesses 41
    1 Advertising Specialties 43
    2 Animal Actors 46
    3 Animal Behavior Therapist 50
    4 Animal Massage Therapist 53
    5 Animal Sounds CD-ROM 56
    6 Ant Colony 59
    7 Aquarium Maintenance 62
    8 Aromatherapist 64
    9 Art Broker 67
    10 Bed and Breakfast 70
    11 Beekeeper 74
    12 Bird Day Care 78
    13 Birding Guides 81
    14 Blacksmith or Farrier 84
    15 Breed Fish 87
    16 Build Designer Dog Houses 90
    17 Build Macquariums 94
    18 Canine Rehabilitation 97
    19 Cat Breeder 101

101 HOME BASED BUSINESSES FOR PET LOVERS

20 Cat Day Care 104
21 Cleaning Bird Cages 106
22 Computer Pet 109
23 Create Paint-By-Numbers Coloring Book 112
24 Critter Products 115
25 Cross Stitch Patterns 119
26 Custom Calendars 122
27 Custom Pet Portraits 125
28 Custom Screen Savers 128
29 Custom Stuffed Animals 130
30 Deliver Kitty Litter 133
31 Designer Jewelry for Pet and Owner 135
32 Dog Cross-Breeder 138
33 Dog Day Care 142
34 Dog Show Handler 145
35 Dog Trainer 149
36 Dog Walker 152
37 DVDs for Pets 155
38 Electronic Dog Trainer 158
39 Embroidery 161
40 Export Consultant 165
41 Fishless Aquarium 169
42 Freelance Riding Instructor 173
43 Freelance Writer 176
44 Geese Patrol 179
45 Grow Worms 183
46 Horse Boarding 186
47 Horse Cargo Trailer Service 190
48 Importer 192
49 Independent Sales Agent 197
50 Install Doggy Doors 201
51 International Pet Travel 203

52 Lease Ecologically Correct Aquariums 207
53 List or Sell Pet Businesses 211
54 Local Portal Website 215
55 Mail Order Supplies 219
56 Make Book Marks 223
57 Make Electronic Photo Albums 227
58 Make Keepsake Pillows 231
59 Mobile Pet Grooming 235
60 Online Dating Service 238
61 Operate a Pet Retirement Home 242
62 Organic Catnip Products 246
63 Paw Casts 248
64 Pet Astrologer 251
65 Pet Bakery 254
66 Pet Carpentry 257
67 Pet Carry All 260
68 Pet Cemetery 263
69 Pet Club of the Month 266
70 Pet Detective 269
71 Pet Food Delivery 271
72 Pet Gift Baskets 274
73 Pet Humor Website 278
74 Pet Insurance 281
75 Pet Party Planner 285
76 Pet Photographer 287
77 Pet Registration 290
78 Pet Referral Service 294
79 Pet Sitting 297
80 Pet Stationery 300
81 Pet Taxi 303
82 Publish Horse Friendly Guide 305
83 Publish Local Pet Newspaper 308

101 Home based Businesses for Pet Lovers

84 Puzzle Maker 311
85 Raise Alpacas 315
86 Raise Birds 319
87 Raise Crickets 323
88 Reminder Service 326
89 Sell Invisible Fencing 330
90 Sell Mobile Bird Cages 332
91 Set Up Koi Ponds 334
92 Show Exotic Pets 338
93 Start Niche Magazine 341
94 Stock Photos and Drawings 345
95 Summer Camp for Dogs 348
96 Tour Operator 351
97 Upscale Pet Products 354
98 Video or DVD Producer 357
99 Virtual Cemetery and Memorial Center 360
100 Write a Guide for Would-Be Breeders 363
101 Yellow Pages Directory 367
Ten Top Tips for Success 370

Before You Start Your Business

Can You Work With the Animals?

It's one thing to sell products or provide services for people with pets. It's another to actually work around animals all day. Many people dream about working surrounded by Fido, Fluffy or Flicka but to ensure the reality doesn't become a nightmare for you, consider:

Do you understand the animals you'll be dealing with?

It's one thing to love Fido or be amused by Fluffy but do you really understand their normal behavior? I can't count how many times I've heard someone complain about a puppy's chewing or a Chihuahua having to go the bathroom so often.

If you haven't worked around animals, volunteer at a local shelter or animal hospital or pet show to become familiar with typical animal behaviors and the variety of behaviors you may encounter.

Do you have any allergies to molds, dust, fur or animal dander?

If you do, consider a business that doesn't require contact with the animals that trigger your allergies. This book describes many businesses that can contribute to the well being of pets without your actual contact with them.

Alternately, do any family members have these allergies? If so, you don't want to start a business that will bring offending allergens into your home.

Do you expect to work regular hours?

Successful pet sitters and animal day care operators work long hours, as do the other business operators who deal with live animals. You can't throw Fido out on the street because his mom or dad is late picking him up from day care.

Think about the schedule and time you want to put into your business. Many businesses dealing with pets are busiest on weekends and holidays.

Are you physically fit for the job?

Working with live animals can require you to move quickly and sometimes to lift or move a recalcitrant pet. You also must be prepared to get down and dirty. If you pale at the thought of picking up pet poop, you're reading the wrong book.

If you're going to work with animals for any length of time, it's likely you're going to get hurt. It may be a scratch; it may be a serious bite that requires hospitalization. You must be prepared for this eventuality and consider how you will deal emotionally, financially and medically with such an eventuality.

Can you travel?

Some of the businesses in this book require traveling or hauling or just driving around town. Consider how much you're willing to do. Traveling also implies getting outside and sometimes that means into the rain, sleet, snow or gloom of night. Is that a problem for you?

Can You Work With the Animals?

Do you need a full-time business with significant income or do you just want to supplement your income with an enjoyable part-time business?

Some businesses can provide a substantial income. Other businesses I describe are more suitable as an income supplement. You need to think about your situation and consider if you can start something new or find a way to segue into the pet business of your dreams.

Once you've answered the above questions, start reviewing the list of businesses to identify the possibilities for you. Many of them can be combined.

I tried to provide enough detail to give you a feel for the business and a list of resources including trade associations so you can research in depth those businesses that most appeal to you.

Now it's up to you!

THREE PLACES TO VISIT BEFORE STARTING YOUR BUSINESS

Your local library

Put your credit card away and take out your library card. To get started, read one or two basic books on starting a home-based business. My suggestions are:

Home Based Businesses for Dummies by Paul and Sarah Edwards, and Peter Economy. Good overview, easy to read. (*For Dummies*, 2000, 359-pages) Available at www.amazon.com for $15.39

Homemade Money. Starting Smart by Barbara Brabec Comprehensive guide by the premier home-business writer (M. Evans and Company, 2003, 335-pages)
Available at www.amazon.com for $17.47

Take advantage of the free resources before buying the magic formula offered on the Internet or in display ads of the business opportunity magazines.

The Internal Revenue Service website

The IRS in conjunction with state and local agencies conducts workshops on starting a new business that include all the information you need to be legal. The workshops can be half-day or full day and either free or with a nominal fee.

Visit this website:

```
http://www.irs.gov/businesses/small/
article/0,,id=99202,00.html
```

Three Places To Visit Before Starting Your Business

to find out when the next one closest to you is scheduled.

Attend a workshop and visit the IRS small business website for more free information on running a small business.

Your state's licensing department

Get legal. If you start an under-the-table business and gain any type of success, you can depend on a competitor turning you in to the authorities. Fines for willful evasion are usually greater than innocent mistakes.

At a minimum, you'll need a business license. If you re-sell products, you'll need a re-sellers certificate so you don't pay sales taxes on the items you intend to resell.

To find out where to check on licensing requirements in your state, visit this website:

http://www.sba.gov/hotlist/license.html

Quick and Easy Way to Keep the Books

One of the saddest things is to see someone become successful, only to go out of business because they weren't tracking cash flow and didn't realize expenses were exceeding income.

Worse, they usually do not have good records for tax purposes and end up owing federal and state taxes.

Use cash record keeping

The simple solution to your bookkeeping is to use cash record keeping. That means you do not record income until you receive it. This system works until you incorporate at which point the IRS requires you to use a more complex system called accrual accounting.

Set up a business checking account

Unlike a personal checking account, you will probably pay a small monthly fee for this although some banks waive fees if you maintain a balance of a certain level. A business account helps convince the IRS that you are operating a legitimate business.

You will need a checkbook and a ledger. Pay all your business bills with checks and document the reason for the payment in the ledger.

Deposit every single cent you take in from your business. Even when you're paid in cash, deposit it all to your checking account. Be sure to write in your ledger what the deposits are for.

Quick and Easy Way to Keep the Books

Then at the end of each month and tax year, you will have a record of all your business income and expenses from your bank. Review your income and outgo each month so you know when you need to make adjustments.

Just think how much easier it will be in April to add the income column and the expense column to determine your tax liability.

Get numbered, multi-part invoices printed with your business name

Office Depot, Costco or Sam's Club can provide invoices or you can use your own laser printer. If your invoices/receipts are numbered, it simplifies tracking invoices to customers. This also helps you identify your major sources of income.

Multi-part means you give one copy to your client and you keep one copy. If you live in a state that requires sales tax, this will help you keep track of how much you will have to pay the state.

Note the invoice number on the deposit record you put in your ledger. This helps track back income to the right customer.

Get a cheap, plastic expansion folder(s) from Office Depot or use several shoe boxes

Use a separate expansion folder for each tax year. Label the divisions with your main categories of business expenses and throw your receipts in there. For instance, pet supplies, advertising, phone, clothing, insurance premiums, professional groups, postage, etc. If you're ever audited, you will need to show receipts.

Keep great track of your automobile expenses

This is a major expense for many businesses. The IRS allows you to deduct actual expenses or standard mileage. If you use the actual expenses method, you must keep EVERY receipt.

Under the mileage approach, you simply total your number of miles driven for business purposes and multiply by the allowed rate for that tax year. You also can deduct highway or bridge tolls and parking fees but not service or repair costs.

It's a good idea to keep minute records and then see which approach works best for you. IRS Publication 463, Travel, Entertainment, Gift, and Car Expenses explains the rules in detail.

Use computer software programs

If you're computer literate, use one of the popular software bookkeeping programs. Many people love Quicken or MYOB (Mind Your Own Business). My favorite is Simply Accounting. All three programs have free demos available at their websites. If you're a sole proprietor, you don't need any software program. You can use Excel to track expenses and income. Once you incorporate or become an LLC, however, you must use an accrual accounting system and that's when these programs become a necessity.

Quick and Easy Way to Keep the Books

Resources

Small Time Operator: How to Start Your Own Business, Keep Your Books, Pay Your Taxes and Stay Out of Trouble!
by Bernard Kamoroff, CPA
(Bell Springs Publishing, 27th ed, 2002, 200-pages)
available at www.amazon.com for $12.57
indexKamoroff, Bernard (bookkeeping)
Software:

Simply Accounting at
http://www.simplyaccounting.com/us/default.asp
Quicken at http://www.quicken.com (offers much free information)
MYOB at http://www.myob.com/us/

Four Marketing Methods You Should Avoid

Don't depend on coupons and discounts to bring you customers

All you will do is bring in the cheapskates, the people who only care about getting the best deal. Quality is not the prime focus for them. They want an OK, or even a so-so, product or service at a bottom-line price.

The people who sell coupons will tell you they're a great way to introduce your product/service to new customers. They're not. Coupon collectors take advantage of the coupon or discount and then move on to the next company that offers one.

Take the money you were going to spend on coupons or discounts and use it to buy bonus products you can give your paying customers. They will be pleased by this thank-you and likely recommend your business to their friends.

Don't set too low a price

When you're starting out and hungry for business, you will be tempted to set a low price with the intention of building business. This doesn't work.

You can't compete on price with Wal-Mart if you're selling products or with someone even hungrier than you if you're selling services.

You don't want the customers who only want cheap. You must offer a best value, meaning the best combination of quality, reliability, and delivery at a reasonable but not cheap price.

Four Marketing Methods You Should Avoid

This is the way to actually make money and build a customer base.

If you start out with a low price, you may find three months into your business that you're losing money or it just isn't worth your time to do it for the small amount you're getting.

You'll probably need to raise your price. This is when you irritate customers. They'll feel you suckered them in with a lowball price or they'll be wondering if you're going to raise prices every other month.

Set a fair price with a good profit margin. It will take time to build your customer base, but it will be a customer base that is becoming loyal to you and one that will hang around as long as you're in business.

Don't create brochures

Most brochures are flimsy, boring products that puff up the ego of the business owner but offer little to customers. How many brochures are in your keepsake drawers?

Brochures are expensive if you want to create an attractive one on quality paper. Is this the best use of your marketing dollars or just a way to make you feel like you're really in business?

People are busy and don't want to read your life story anyway. Instead, develop your "unique selling proposition." That's the one sentence that describes what you can do for your customer. Put that sentence on your business card.

Let your competitors waste their money on four-color brochures.

Don't use search engine placement software

If you're going to have a website, you need to be listed in Google and the other search engines. Unfortunately, this is an area ripe with scam artists and products that don't work.

Submit your website manually and individually to all the search engines. All of them have guidelines on how to get listed. For instance, check out *http://www.google.com/addurl.html* on getting listed at Google, an absolute must.

Typically, someone figures out how to game Google, sells his information to other webmasters and all benefit—for a while. Then a competitor complains to Google who knocks out the web pages or penalizes them in rankings.

There are two search engine experts I can recommend as being both knowledgeable and ethical. Both offer free e-mail newsletters on search engine positioning:

Jill Whalen at HighRankings.com
http://www.highrankings.com/

Sean Burns at WebmastersReference.com
http://www.webmastersreference.com/

Nine Marketing Methods You Should Use

Flyers

They're inexpensive to make and can be left at other businesses, homes, community centers, grocery store bulletin boards, and anywhere else you can leave them.

Just make certain you target an upscale area that can afford your service or product and that has pets. The county or city office that processes dog and cat licenses may make names and addresses of license holders available to the public or sell them for a nominal fee.

If you have a photograph of your product or service, incorporate it into the flyer.

Create a good one by —

Using all capital letters with no underlining or bold type.

Saying in two or three lines what you can do for the customer.

If appropriate, offering a free estimate. CALL ME FOR A NO OBLIGATION ESTIMATE.

If you will be doing your business in or at a customer's home, noting that you're LICENSED, BONDED, INSURED (if that's true, and it should be).

If you don't need a full page (e.g., you don't have a product to show or a before and after picture), dividing the page into three rows of equal size and create three flyers from one page.

101 Home based Businesses for Pet Lovers

Signing your name on each of the flyers individually or by using a font that looks like handwriting. It suggests a note to a homeowner or customer rather than an advertising circular.

Business cards using Rolodex card stock

Have your type of business printed on the index tab. For instance, Pet Sitter.

The body of the Rolodex card is your normal contact information and if there's room, a sentence about your best benefit.

Magnets with your contact information

This is good if your customers are at home and unlikely to have a Rolodex. Hand out a refrigerator magnet in a shape that makes sense for your business; e.g., a bone, a horse or a computer with your contact information. Always leave one when you finish a job.

Car signs, either painted on the car or magnetic signs

Your car can be a rolling billboard. Have your business name and phone number or URL painted on your car, or use a magnetic sign that can be attached to your car. One caveat—check with your auto insurance agent to make sure advertising on your car is legal and won't violate your insurance policy.

Postcards rather than letters for mail marketing

Direct mail can be effective if it's targeted and the message is clear. I like to use postcards with photographs (you buy them ready made) and then have your message printed on the postcard. Postage for postcards is considerably cheaper than letters, and you avoid the additional cost of envelopes.

Nine Marketing Methods You Should Use

Postcards are good when you're contacting existing or prior customers about a new service or product. They also can be used in lieu of newsletters and brochures.

Marketing calendar

Have a calendar and on each workday (Monday through Friday) write down a marketing tool or technique that you're going to do that day. Line through it when you're done.

For instance:

- Monday send press release to local newspaper.

- Tuesday visit veterinarian offices within a 5-block radius and leave business cards, flyers or whatever there.

- Wednesday visit three apartment or condominium offices and leave marketing materials.

Each day does not have to be a major undertaking. The goal is to do something each workday (you can relax on weekends and do your paperwork!) and to write it down.

Plan your week in advance. You must market FOREVER to keep a good customer base.

If you do this, you will be ahead of 99% of your competitors. Most people will not create written goals or they start off strong but ask so much of themselves that they can't keep up, get depressed and quit.

One final tip—always include your URL, if you have a website, on every marketing material, letter, packing slip, invoice and anything that can hold a URL on it.

Kits

Develop a kit for the type of pet you deal with or for several types of pets if you have a more general business. These can be sold at holidays for gifts or to new pet owners.

An example is a kit for new aquarium owners with cleaning materials, filters, fish food, water conditioner, heater and thermometer. Offer three different priced kits—a basic, a moderate and a premium one. You'll be surprised how popular these can be.

Word of Mouth

There's no better publicity or marketing than having satisfied customers recommend your product or service to their friends and neighbors. Do reward customers who send you business.

You can give them a bonus the next time they buy or use your product or service.Or, give them a clever gift. One colleague gives back scratchers with the printed message: "Thanks for scratching my back. HendersonPetSitters.com."

This encourages recommendations while rewarding your loyal customers. What could be better?

State Your Price

If your business lends itself to set prices; e.g., pet sitter or acquarium maintenance, develop a price schedule and include it with your marketing materials. I recommend creating a bookmark size insert with your price schedule, by the hour or day or service. At least give a range if you can't give specific prices.

Be sure to include the right to amend the price for services beyond normal range and include an expiration date for your

Nine Marketing Methods
You Should Use

price schedule. For instance, "Prices good through 31 December 2004." You don't want someone 10-years from now finding your price schedule and demanding you clean their bird cage for $5.

You will hear people refute this, but as a customer, I feel if someone doesn't state a price it's because they're so expensive. I don't call to ask for a price because I don't want a heavy sales push. Stating prices helps customers select themselves and avoids wasting your time with people who can't afford or won't pay your prices.

Care and Feeding of Clients and Customers

When you need to have a client meeting

It's doubtful if you want strangers coming into your home, even when they're potential customers. For those occasions when you need to meet with them and can't use their office (or home), there are some alternatives to consider:

A. Lunch—meet at a family-type restaurant such as Marie Callender's or other chain

B. Public library—many have meeting rooms that are free or at a nominal charge

C. Kinkos—many of the branches even offer videoconferencing rooms

D. Executive suites—there are many commercial businesses today that rent out offices and provide office administration services. Check your telephone book.

The customer is not always right, but he's always the customer

I hope you enjoy all types of people because you're likely to run into many of them. Try to remember that you wouldn't have a business if it weren't for them. When a nitwit tries your patience or a arrogant jerk acts condescendingly, mentally take a deep breath and think, "You're making my house payment; I can stand you."

Care and Feeding
of Clients and Customers

On the other hand, don't be afraid to fire a customer

Some people can't be pleased and you will spend too much time and emotional energy finding that out. When you've done your best and the customer isn't happy, give up. Yes, give up. Tell the customer it's unfortunate but you do not seem to be the right dog walker, horse trainer, photographer or whatever for them, and you hope they find someone more suited for their business. Never blame the customer, no matter how much they deserve it. Be professional and say good-bye as calmly and politely as possible.

Some people will haggle forever on price—if you let them

There are plenty of cheapskates out there who will try to get something for nothing. There's nothing wrong with negotiating, but you will soon learn the difference. As I mentioned in an earlier chapter, I will not use discounts or coupons to get customers. If a customer claims that a competitor would provide your product or service for a cheaper price, just smile and say, "They know what they're worth." If that doesn't work, then read the paragraph above on firing a customer.

Some people will cheat you

New business people often feel cheated by customers who buy and use their product or service and then try to get their money back. Get over it.

A friend who sells manuals often gets requests for refunds with his customer returning a copy of the manual rather than the manual. In one case, the customer left the Kinko's invoice for copying right in the manual! What did my friend do? He immediately refunded the money.

Repeat: "it's not personal, it's business." You must have enough margins in your prices to cover this.

Most importantly, however, don't continue to do business with a customer who owes you money. Get a deposit if not payment-in-full before you begin any work. Remember the old saying: fool me once, shame on you; fool me twice, shame on me.

Honor money back guarantees—whether you have one or not

New business people often do not want to offer any money-back guarantees because they think it will encourage the crooks like the one who cheated my friend above. That's very possible BUT you need to understand the laws of your state and the rules of your merchant credit card account or third-party credit card provider.

Customers buy from strangers over the Internet and in stores because they know they can get their money back if they are cheated because they used a credit card to pay for it. You may see this operate unfairly as credit card providers always take the customer's side even in the face of documented counter-evidence.

Be glad. If they didn't, who would ever buy from new or small businesses? Yes, the system can be unfair in an individual instance but overall it works to your advantage.

Guarantees or warranties may be required by your state or locality

Regarding guarantees, many states and localities are requiring businesses to refund money if a customer asks for it within a certain time limit. Even if your state doesn't require this, when someone asks for his or her money back, REFUND IT.

Care and Feeding
of Clients and Customers

There are many hysterical people out there. If they feel they didn't get their money's worth, they will seek vengeance. I've seen people write their Congressman; file complaints with the U.S. Postal Service, State Attorney General, Federal Trade Commission, Better Business Bureau; and flame the business on Internet discussion boards when the money involved was less than $20. Truly.

It isn't worth dealing with a nut. Unfair or not, if you accumulate too many complaints, your state Attorney General may launch an investigation of your business. That is worse than losing one sale.

Remember, your job is to make money for you and your family. Your job is not to right the world's wrongs or try to control hysterical nitwits with more time than brains.

When you're getting too many refund requests

If your requests for refunds are growing or a high percentage (double digits), you need to examine whether the problem is a) your product or b) your market.

It's unusual for a pet sitter to get many refund requests, but it happens all the time to Internet marketers who sell the "Follow My Plan and Make a Million Dollars This Week."

The "Make Millions" product attracts problematic people: the crooks and the naive. The outright crooks just want to copy the plan, return it for a refund and then resell it as their own. The incredibly naive are looking for that magic potion that enables them to make millions with no work. When they see this isn't a magic wand, they feel cheated and demand their money back.

Take a look at your product or service first and ask customers -both those who returned it and those who didn't-to provide feedback and suggestions for improvement. Don't rely on your family or friends who may not want to hurt your feelings.

Once you're confident your product or service is worthwhile, then look at your marketing. Target the groups that not only want your product or service but can pay for it. Target them in the geographic locations or advertising media they frequent.

Most importantly, don't target people with low or no incomes. As the old saying goes, if you are going after customers with no money, that is what you're likely to get - no money.

Four Most Trying Legal Issues

Zoning Laws and Homeowners Association Rules

Many cities and homeowners associations have restrictive laws and rules that prohibit any commercial activity in the home. You will need to visit your community's zoning office and find out what is permitted and what is not. If you have a homeowners association, review the bylaws.

Expect your neighbors to complain if you have numerous strange animals or people coming to your home, make a lot of noise or create odors with your business, or take up all the parking spaces with delivery trucks and customer cars.

On the other hand, if your business is solitary or you use your home just as the administrative office, you shouldn't have any problems with the neighbors.

Many home-based business owners get a mailbox at a commercial company such as Pony Express and use that address as their business address, even for their business license although most states forbid that.

The only good news is that homeowners are rarely fined for zoning violations. The city or county sends a cease-and-desist letter and if the homeowner stops the unlawful activity, that usually ends it.

Your homeowners association is a different issue. Try to maintain a good relationship with the board and even serve on it if you can. Homeowners groups can be good or bad depending on how cliquish and rigid the members are.

101 Home based Businesses for Pet Lovers

Insurance

You will need liability insurance. This is especially important if you work with live animals and/or if you enter people's homes as part of your business. If your business has a trade association, see if it offers a group policy. Also check out your local Chamber of Commerce. Many Chambers offer reasonable group policies including health insurance.

Your homeowners or renters insurance probably does not cover any business you operate in your home. In fact, if you start a business and the UPS driver trips on your stairs making a delivery, your insurance carrier may deny the claim because you've violated the terms of your policy.

You must be honest with your insurance agent about your business. Some insurance companies offer an umbrella policy or rider for home-based businesses.

Many companies do not like to insure home businesses that involve live animals even harmless ones like ladybugs. One source to keep in mind is the Farm Bureau in your state. See your yellow pages or contact your county extension service.

You need computer insurance. If you use your computer for your business, that also probably violates the terms of your homeowners or renter's insurance policy. You may need a separate policy (see www.safeware.com) or a rider for your policy.

If you use your vehicle in your business, make certain your policy covers this and if you put advertising on your vehicle, make sure your policy permits that. Ask your agent.

Frivolous lawsuits

Four Most Trying Legal Issues

Some lawyers in California have formed for-profit organizations that do nothing but sue small businesses. (Large businesses can afford to counter sue and retaliate).

For example, one law firm specialized in suing nail salons because the salons weren't opening new bottles of nail polish for each client. The law firm claimed the salons were violating consumer protection laws but offered to drop the lawsuit if the nail salons would pay them a few thousand dollars.

The best way to avoid inane lawsuits is to elect Congressional and state legislators who vote for tort reform and cap settlements.

The next best way is to use a business arrangement to shield your assets. This is the main reason people stop doing business as a sole proprietorship and incorporate or establish a Limited Liability Company (LLC).

Corporate requirements

You certainly should consider incorporating or operating as an LLC; however, be aware that a corporate structure requires a significant commitment to administrative matters and is subject to other states rules. If you fail to keep your paperwork in order, a state court may set aside your corporate status and hold you individually responsible for your business debts.

Even if you incorporate as a one-person business, in some states every corporation or LLC must have an employee (you as president and janitor) and must contribute to the state unemployment compensation and workmen's compensation insurance plans. Those can be expensive. You need to check this out with your Secretary of State and at the free IRS workshops mentioned in the *Three Places To Visit Before Starting Your Business* chapter.

If you perform a service and have no employees and no products, it may be more reasonable to shield your assets rather than the business and rely on an umbrella insurance policy for your business.

Rather than incorporating your business, put your home or other property within a family trust or LLC or corporation so that those assets can't be used to pay off any lawsuits your business incurs. Check with a local lawyer on the best way to separate them from your business assets. One good website for publications on legal issues associated with running a business is Nolo at `http://www.nolo.com`.

FOUR ETHICAL CONCERNS

Exotic pets

You may recall the 2003 outbreak of monkeypox, a viral disease similar to smallpox, transmitted by some prairie dogs that were purchased as pets. This re-ignited the debate over whether anyone needs to keep exotic pets such as rodents and poisonous snakes. In many areas, including the state of California, it's still illegal to keep ferrets as pets because they're considered disease-carrying rodents.

If you live in an area that has laws against rodents or other animals as pets and you don't exclude those animals from your customer base, you may inadvertently negate your business liability insurance coverage by engaging in an unlawful activity. Check your policy and ask your agent.

I'm not going to try to tell you what to do. Just consider whether you want to handle exotic pets or provide products or services for their owners.

Breeding

Several businesses in this book describe various types of breeding businesses.

There are those, however, who believe that no species is more important, or should have greater rights than another. They do not believe human beings have the right to make a pet of any animal.

You often will hear complaints about too many dogs already in shelters. Note that in most parts of the country there is a shortage of small dogs and puppies in shelters. Some shelters actually import small dogs from third-world countries to meet demand. Most of the dogs in shelters are large dogs and adult dogs that have behavior problems. It's sad but visit your own county's animal shelter and see what you find there.

Guardianship vs. Ownership

Some well-meaning and some not well-meaning people want to change the laws so that pet owners are termed "guardians."

The animal rights groups want pet ownership to be as difficult and expensive as possible because they don't believe any human has a right to make an animal a pet.

Law firms are looking for a new market for lawsuits. If you are the "guardian" rather than the "owner" of a pet, you may be held to a higher standard of behavior and subjected to possible lawsuits by groups representing your pet.

If a pet is owned, he's considered property under the law, and there's no pain and suffering for an injured pet. On the other hand, if a pet is under a guardianship, there is no monetary limit on damages.

I'm not encouraging or excusing irresponsible behavior, but I am asking you to be realistic.

A dog is going to act like a dog. No matter how careful a dog walker might be, it is possible and likely that, at some point, some dog will break away and attack another dog.

Should the other dog's owner be entitled to millions of dollars (think McDonalds coffee cup) for emotional distress? Or, is it reasonable to just reimburse the owner for actual expenses? Think about the consequences of innocuous sounding legislation and make up your own mind.

Four Ethical Concerns

Domestic terrorists

Violence is a tactic of some animal rights groups. Bombs have been detonated at laboratories that use animals for research and fires have been started in fast food restaurants that serve meat. If you doubt how crazy and dangerous these groups can be, visit the Animal Liberation Front website or its sibling group, the Earth Liberation Front.

In addition to overt violence, these groups practice intimidation by posting names, phone numbers and addresses of their opponents on websites, hoping that nuts will harass these people.

A consumer group has asked the Internal Revenue Service to revoke the non-profit status of People for the Ethical Treatment of Animals (PETA) because of its financial contributions to the Earth Liberation Front and the Animal Liberation Front. It's easy to think of PETA as a group of harmless Hollywood airheads, but PETA collects millions of dollars in donations each year. Yet, for example, PETA has used its tax-free dollars for a legal defense fund for an arsonist who pled guilty to setting a fire at Michigan State University research lab.

Before you advocate or financially support any animal rights group, do some research at the website
`http://www.naiaonline.org`
of the National Animal Interest Alliance. You might be unpleasantly surprised at what you learn there.

You need to think about protecting yourself and your business if you deal with live animals.

Resources Every Pet Business Should Know

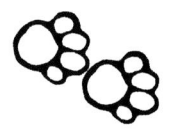

American Red Cross Pet First Aid Course and Manual

This national organization offers a course in first aid for dogs and cats and sells a first aid manual. The course is offered at a nominal fee (usually less than $25) and the manual sells for $19.95. Unfortunately, not every Red Cross offers this, but please check one near you. This is a great course for anyone who works with dogs or cats or has one as a pet.

Also, the Red Cross needs volunteers to be trained to teach the course. Being a certified Red Cross Pet First Aid instructor is a nice addition to your resume and a worthwhile way for you to make a contribution to the pet community.

Visit their website at

http://www.redcross.org/services/hss/courses/pets.html.

Internet Clip Art

Microsoft Office Online Offers a superb collection of clip art that can be used, but not sold, on websites. It's difficult to find quality clip art on the Internet that you can use, confident that you're not violating any copyrights. This satisfies both those concerns.

http://office.microsoft.com/clipart/default.aspx.

Resources Every Pet Business Should Know

Information and Help

County Extension Services offers free help and publications (free or at a nominal cost) on all agricultural related topics including animals. Offices are usually located in conjunction with a state university, especially the Agriculture or Farming department. The offices are funded in part by the U.S. Department of Agriculture.

Check the government section of your phone book to locate one.

Magazines

There are three monthly magazines devoted to the broad pet industry. All three offer free subscriptions to legitimate pet businesses.

Pet Product News
http://www.petproductnews.com
P.O. Box 6050
Mission Viejo, CA 92690-6050
Phone: 949.855.8822

Pet Business
http://www.petbusiness.com
333 Seventh Avenue, 11th Floor
New York, NY 10001
Phone: 212.979.4800

Pet Age
http://www.petage.com/
H.H. Backer Associates Inc.
200 S. Michigan Ave., Suite 840
Chicago, IL 60604

101 Home based Businesses for Pet Lovers

Phone: 312.663.4040

Marketing Materials and Legal Forms

Microsoft Office Online Templates: Whenever you're looking for a template for a mailing, letter, legal form, even a food diary if you've been snacking too much at home, check out Microsoft. They have a wonderful collection of templates that are free to use.

http://office.microsoft.com/templates/default.aspx?CTT=6&Origin=EC790020111033

Marketing—Media and Customers

Standard Rate and Data Services (SRDS): Comprehensive listing of places to advertise or send press releases. Equally important, summarizes the available mailing lists of people who have recently purchased products associated with all types of pets or pet care. This is super expensive so see if you can gain access through your library system. SRDS also publishes hard copy volumes that your library may carry.

Suppliers

The three magazines listed above all publish annual collections of pet product manufacturers. In the meantime, if you need to locate an address for a manufacturer or identify a company that will make your product, the best resource is *The Thomas Register*.

Visit your library to review a hard copy or go to their website at http://www.thomasregister.com, which is open to subscribers. A subscription is expensive so see if your library system has one or use the hard copy volumes.

Resources Every Pet Business Should Know

Trade Groups

American Pet Products Manufacturers Association (APPMA)
www.appma.org/
255 Glenville Road Greenwich, CT 06831
Phone: 203.532.0000

National Animal Interest Alliance
(only $35 a year and worth it)
Advocacy for pet ownership and resource
on animal rights extremists
http://www.naiaonline.org/
P.O. Box 66579
Portland, OR 97290-6579

Pet Industry Distributors Association
(wholesalers and distributors)
http://www.pida.org/
2105 Laurel Bush Road, Suite 200
Bel Air, MD 21015
Phone: 443.640.1060

Pet Industry Joint Advisory Council (PIJAC)
Highly recommended for all.
Offers certification programs, education and advocacy of
pet businesses
http://www.pijac.org/i4a/pages/index.cfm?pageid=1
1220 19th Street, NW, Suite 400
Washington, DC 20036
Phone: 202.452.1525

Trade Shows

Show your products or see what's new in the industry.

H.H. Backer Associates sponsors two major trade shows: Backer's annual Spring and annual Christmas Trade Show and Educational Conference.

Learn more at `http://www.hhbacker.com` or contact

H.H. Backer Associates Inc.
200 S. Michigan Ave., Suite 840
Chicago, IL 60604
Phone: 312.663.4040

Trade Show—Largest

Largest industry show is the joint American Pet Products Manufacturers Association (APPMA) at `http://www.appma.org` and the Pet Industry Distributors Association (PIDA) at *http://www.pida.org*.

Visit:
`http://www.pida.org/joint_tradeshow_agreement.html` for information on the new joint show. The first one will be March 13-15, 2005 at the Orange County Convention Center in Orlando, FL. Addresses for both industry groups are in listings of Trade Groups

101 Home-Based Businesses

1   Advertising Specialties

General Concept

You sell advertising or marketing products to pet related businesses. These products include refrigerator magnets, calendars, Post-It notes and anything else that can hold a company name and contact information. For example, envision a bone-shaped refrigerator magnet with the name, address and phone number of a dog groomer.

Profit Potential

You earn commissions on products sold. Kaesar & Blair, the leading distributor, estimates agents who work diligently should be earning $30,000 to $50,000 by their second year.

Equipment Needed

Get a re-sellers certificate from your state so you don't have to pay sales tax when you buy a product intended for re-sell. Sign up for the Kaesar and Blair distributorship through BASSCO (see Resources). This will give you support from a very successful agent. The fee to get started with Kaesar and Blair in 2004 is $85 and includes numerous sample products as well as marketing materials.

You are not limited to selling only Kaesar and Blair products, and you may expand your line when you're ready. I recommend starting with this company, however, because it doesn't require a major financial investment, but it will provide you the opportunity to see if you like this business and want to stay with it.

101 Home based Businesses for Pet Lovers

Getting Started

Arrange your samples in some type of binder or portfolio case and take them around to local pet-related businesses.

Have some products, with you name and contact information including e-mail and URL if you have a website, that you can leave with potential customers. Recommended products are those that a customer is likely to keep such as a Rolodex card rather than pens or pencils that tend to get lost rapidly. Create a website with your products but don't expect to be able to build a business solely using the Internet. You must get out and knock on doors (figuratively speaking) to build a customer base.

Offer to trade advertising specialties for the cost of ads in newspapers, on radio stations and a local Yellow Page listing. A well-done ad in the Yellow Pages can bring in sales as long as you haven't had to pay too much for it. Display ads in most Yellow Pages cost several hundred dollars a *month.*

Pitfalls to Avoid

Have a local lawyer look over any contract you plan to sign to become an independent distributor. You don't want to inadvertently become liable for taxes in your home state if the company you represent fails to pay state sales taxes or other fees. It is not unheard of for a state to go over a local agent if the manufacturer or wholesaler resides elsewhere.

Also read the chapter in this book on Independent Sales Agents.

Growth Potential & Expansion

Join local Chambers of Commerce and network continually.

Advertising Specialties

Competition

If you can sell face-to-face, you never have to worry about competition; there will always be room in any market for you.

Keys to Success

Help customers envision how the product(s) would look in their store and how it will help them sell more merchandise.

Resources

BASSCO, Inc, authorized dealer for Kaeser and Blair
with a mentoring program
http://www.cuttingedgeadvertising.com/
Phone: 337.527.8717

The Advertising Specialty Institute (premier trade association)
http://www.joinasi.com/dist/index.htm
4800 Street Road
Trevose, PA 19053
For membership information, e-mail: info@asicentral.com
There are various requirements, including evidence of sales made,
for membership.

Promotional Products Association International (PPAI)
Offers educational and certification programs but also has dollar threshold of sales to become a member.
http://www.ppai.org/
3125 Skyway Circle N
Irving, TX 75038

http://www.promomart.com/
Online mall of promotional products, possibly world's largest.

2 Animal Actors

General Concept

Does your doghouse have a Brad Pittbull or Marilyn Muttroe? Could your pet be on television or in the movies? One retired police-dog handler now provides dogs for TV shows and earns about $34,000 a year. Even if you don't live in Los Angeles or New York, your pet might be able to do print or TV commercials for local advertising agencies.

Profit Potential

Unless you're lucky enough to have a pet become a regular on a TV show, this is a part-time business that's as much about loving the pets and getting to travel with them as making money. Animals typically earn $150 to $2,500 a day depending on what they're asked to do.

Of course, on the other hand, if you get a hit show, you can be set for life. TV show regulars, even canine or feline, can make a six-figure income. This, however, is as likely as winning the lotto.

Equipment Needed

Just your normal pet handling equipment plus dependable transportation.

You will need a talent agent to help find jobs and negotiate with production companies. Use your local yellow pages but do NOT pay any agency to get listed.

Animal Actors

Getting Started

If your pet doesn't know hand signals, train him in the basic commands using signals. Remember the owner/trainer is off camera and needs to communicate with his pet while the pet's on camera.

Get some professional photographs and/or video of your pet ready to submit to talent agents and local advertising agencies. Call the agency and find out what type of submission they want.

Try to get on Animal Planet (see Resources). This TV channel has a wide range of opportunities and a need for all types of pets either in person or on tape.

Pitfalls to Avoid

Don't try to make your pet do anything he doesn't want to do and don't use harsh methods to correct or train him. No reputable agent or producer will work with an owner who mistreats his animals.

Growth Potential & Expansion

Add to your stable with more pets in your specialty or branch out to rarer species. If you succeed in getting a producer to use one of your pets and the experience is good, it's likely the producer will call on you again when he needs another pet.

Competition

Very competitive with many adorable pets looking for jobs.

Keys to Success

Most crucial is having a thoroughly socialized animal with an easy-going disposition. Training is important but remember,

TV pets just have to look like they're accomplishing a task; they don't really have to do it. Your pet must respond to basic hand signals but does not need to be at the level of a companion-animal or police dog.

What can't be faked is having your pet work well other actors, humans as well as animal. Your pet may come into contact with any type of person—young, old, white, black, in uniform, running, male, female, on bikes, etc.—and must interact with them without problems. Dogs must be reliable off-leash.

Most animals that get work are very easy to work with, as are their owners.

ANIMAL ACTORS

Resources

Boone's Animals for Hollywood, Inc.
(premier dog provider in Hollywood)
http://www.boonesanimals.com/
31550 Oakhorn Ave.
Castaic, CA 91384
Phone: 661.257.0630

Animal Planet
http://animal.discovery.com/
features/getonshow/getonshow.html

As I wrote this, Animal Planet was paying $100 for tapes of funny animals and starting interviews in Los Angeles for pets with interesting stories.

How to Get Your Pet into Show Business
(out-of-print book)
by Arthur J. Haggerty
(Hungry Minds, Inc, 1994)
available through used book dealers and
http://www.fetchbooks.info

Star Pet: How to Make Your Pet a Star
by Bash Dibra
more information at
http://www.starpet.com

3 Animal Behavior Therapist

General Concept

Why is Fido or Fluffy or Slinky acting the way he is? If you have an affinity for animals and believe you intuitively understand them, this may be the right business for you. Owners of expensive animals such as horses or show dogs and owners of beloved pets will be your clients.

WARNING: More and more states license and regulate animal therapists. Make sure you meet your state's requirements before you advertise your services. Some people prefer to call themselves a "pet psychologist" and if your state permits this and you have a degree in psychology, that's a possibility.

Profit Potential

Charge $50-200 per consultation, depending on your locality.

Equipment Needed

True professional animal therapists have advanced degrees: BA/BS in either biology or psychology and then a Ph.D. in Animal Behavior. Others – provided this satisfies your state laws – have two-year degrees for animal veterinary technician or assistant with a 4-year degree in psychology. Check with your local community colleges and universities for what programs they offer if you don't meet state requirements.

Other equipment, depending on your specialty, should be less than $200 for things like leads and head halters. You will need dependable transportation to get to client appointments.

Animal Behavior Therapist

You also will need insurance including malpractice insurance. Look at umbrella policies for home businesses.

Getting Started

Get certified and if your state requires it, get licensed. Then specialize in one type of animal (e.g., dogs, cats, horses or exotic pets).

Animal therapists should join the Animal Behavior Society at Indiana University ($51 a year) and get certified from it. Certification requires a minimum of 7 years total of education and/or experience.

Advertise in any local pet publications and leave flyers at shows for the type of pet you specialize in – horse shows, cat shows or dog shows, etc.

Pitfalls to Avoid

Don't run afoul of any state laws and don't make promises you may not be able to keep.

Animals are inherently unpredictable; you're only human. Do not make a promise or offer a guarantee. If you bring patients (i.e., animals) into your home, make sure you obey local zoning ordinances and have sufficient parking space for the animal owners so your neighbors do not complain to authorities.

Growth Potential & Expansion

Write books, offer seminars, become a teacher at an accredited school.

Competition

Not many people specialize in this.

101 Home based Businesses for Pet Lovers

Keys to Success

Do a good job and get referrals. I can't stress how important it is to be able to communicate with animals (I really think it is an innate gift that can be honed not infused by education). Specialize in certain breeds or types of animals. It's easier to get well known in horse circles if you only do horses. The same is true of other animals.

Resources

Animal Behavior Society
Indiana University
2611 East 10th Street #170
Bloomington, IN 47408-2603
Phone: 812-856-5541

Memoirs of a Pet Therapist
by Denise Madden
(Random House, Inc., 1998, 258-pages).
Based on the work of Warren Eckstein, a renowned animal therapist.

Example of animal therapist business:
Animal Behavior Associates, Inc.
http://www.animalbehaviorassociates.com/
4994 South Independence Way
Littleton, CO 80123
Phone: 303.932.9095

4   Animal Massage Therapist

General Concept

A common practice in the horseracing industry, animal massage is starting to make its way into the lives of household pets especially with the growing interest in holistic veterinary medicine.

At the same time, more states are beginning to license and regulate animal massage therapists.

As this is a newer concept, some states have required massage therapy to be done under the supervision of a veterinarian; thereby limiting the ability of animal massage therapists to have their own practices. Most states, however, are letting massage therapists have their own practice provided they meet the state educational and experience requirements.

It is your responsibility to find out what your state laws are and to ensure you meet them before you advertise your services.

Remember: it would be easy to damage an already sick animal, if you don't know what you're doing with the massage.

Profit Potential

Charge $50-100 per consultation, depending on your locality. Beverly Hills, CA therapists charge more than Des Moines, IA therapists.

Equipment Needed

Hone your natural desire with some professional training and a certificate or degree.

More and more schools are offering massage therapy courses. For instance, the University of Nevada at Las Vegas offers a 200-hour certification program to become an animal massage practitioner and is a leader in this field. With tuition and other expenses, you could spend $2,000 to get the required education.

States are imposing rigid standards to license animal massage practitioners. For instance, in the state of Alabama: "Before performing therapeutic massage on an animal, a massage therapist shall graduate from a nationally approved program and complete at least 100 hours of postgraduate training and education in animal anatomy, pathology, and physiology for the type of animal upon which the massage therapist wishes to perform therapeutic massage."

Other equipment, depending on your specialty, should be less than $200 for things like leads and head halters and essential oils for massages. You'll need a massage table, if you do small animals, that you can probably get used.

Getting Started

Get certified and if your state requires it, get licensed. Then specialize in one type of animal (e.g., dogs, cats, horses or exotic pets). Volunteer your services at a local animal shelter to gain experience.

Once you meet your state's laws, advertise in any local pet publications and leave flyers at shows for the type of pet you specialize in—horse shows, cat shows or dog shows, etc.

Pitfalls to Avoid

Don't make promises or guarantees. Animals are unpredictable. Don't run afoul of any state laws and if you bring patients (i.e.,

Animal Massage Therapist

animals) into your home, make sure you obey local ordinances and have sufficient parking space for the owners so your neighbors do not complain to authorities.

Growth Potential & Expansion

Write books, offer seminars, become a teacher at an accredited school.

Competition

Not many people specialize in this although it's becoming trendy.

Keys to Success

Do a good job and get referrals. Specialize in certain breeds or types of animals. It's easier to get well known in horse circles if you only do horses. The same is true of other animals.

Resources

National Certification Board for Therapeutic
Massage and Bodywork
8201 Greensboro Drive, Suite 300
McLean, VA 22102
Phone: 703.610.9015

Example of animal massage therapist:
http://www.treetops.on.ca/
Treetops Animal Care
6487 3rd Line, R.R. #2,
Alliston, Ontario, Canada L9R 1V2
Phone: 705.435.6174

5 Animal Sounds CD-ROM

General Concept

You record the sounds of some type of animal—birds, crickets, cats, and geese, whatever—to create a CD-ROM of sounds that you sell. These are natural, soothing sounds for many people who want to create a country environment even though they're living in an urban area.

Profit Potential

CD-ROMs typically sell for $10 to $20 but cost less than $4 to make and package.

Equipment Needed

Get a mini-disc recorder or use the audio ability of your video camera if you own one. Make sure your mini-disc recorder can adjust the recording level on the fly and jump to the next recording rather than recording over previous recordings. (The sales staff at Radio Shack can help select one.)

You need a computer that can create CD-ROMs or you need to use a commercial audio recording service. If you do your own labels, you need an inkjet or laser color printer.

Getting Started

Take your recorder to the area where the animals are you want to record and record them at various times during the day. Avoid background noises and stay far enough away from the recorder so that it doesn't pick up any sounds from you, such as shuffling your feet or coughing.

Animal Sounds CD-ROM

Once you have a nice assortment, transfer them onto your computer and then burn a CD-ROM. You can make individual copies or take the master to an audio recording service. For CD-ROM labels, you can use a kit to create them. Good products are NEATO and CD Stomper, both available at office supply stores.

Pitfalls to Avoid

Make sure your CD-ROM can be played in any computer or CD player. Test one on as many friends' equipment as you can.

Do not record with a CD-R. With a digital mini-disc recorder, every copy you make will be crisp, you can edit on the mini-disc and it can be "written" on many times without degrading performance.

Growth Potential & Expansion

Expand your line. If you started with one type of bird, add two or three other species.

If you're technically oriented, you can create audios that customers can download from the Internet for a fee. The problem is that many customers do not understand how to do this or have their computer set up properly so you must provide technical assistance. Downloading music or sounds is easier with a youth-market rather than an adult market as is likely to be the case for natural animal sounds.

Competition

There are natural-sounding CD-ROMs available but most include some type of musical background. One line has wind chimes and woodwind instruments while another has seagulls and waves with a classical symphony in the background. These

101 Home based Businesses for Pet Lovers

are nice but distinguish your product by just being the natural animal sound without artificial enhancements. Many people like to fall asleep to the sound of seagulls or loons.

Keys to Success

You can sell these by consignment, leaving them at pet, feed or bird stores on a rack you supply (available from office supply stores) or sell in bulk directly to the stores.

Don't overlook selling them on the Internet and if you want to go to the expense of getting an Universal Product Codes (UPCs) that is bar-coded you can have your CD-ROM listed for sale at amazon.com and other book or record stores (see Resources). Also offer them for sale at eBay.

Resources

Uniform Code Council Inc.
http://www.uc-council.org/
8163 Old Yankee Road, Suite J
Dayton, OH 45458 USA
Phone: 937.435.3870

For some examples:
Thayer Birding Software Nature Store
(top provider of bird CD-ROMs)
http://www.withoutbricks.com/estore/default.asp?affiliate=thayerbirding

Zooish Animal Sounds
(includes cats, dogs, insects, penguins, etc.) A must visit!
http://www.zooish.com/

6 ANT COLONY

General Concept

You build and sell an ant colony. These aren't real colonies, just containers of some design that house ants.

Ant colonies aren't as popular as they once were, but they still captivate many children once they've seen them.

More surprisingly, there are many adult hobbyists who have ant colonies, some very elaborate ones. Ants are the world's tiniest engineers and many people love to watch them dig tunnels, build roads and erect bridges.

Two notes: 1) the official name for the study of ants is myrmecology and 2) the term "ant farm" is a trademark of Uncle Milton Industries. Don't use it for your own advertising.

Profit Potential

One company sells a small, dome shaped ant home for $18 with $8 refill kits of 25 ants and markets these to elementary school children. Replacement kits are a great idea as the ants typically live only one to four months because there's no queen to lay eggs and hatch new workers.

Larger ant colonies usually sell around $30 while the Uncle Milton original ant farm is about $12 (see Resources).

Equipment Needed

Decide what type of home you want to create for them and then buy your ants (about $3 for 25 harvester ants) or seek them out in their natural habitat; e.g., logs. Most commercial ant colonies are leaf-cutter ants or harvester ants.

You can't buy queen ants commercially as it is illegal to sell them in the U.S. You'll need to find one in nature (good luck in recognizing one) or find a local hobbyist through classifieds at websites such as Ant Colony Developers Association to help you acquire one. Your colony (and business) won't last long without a queen.

Getting Started

Read up on ants so you understand how to care for them and the best types for your business.

Send flyers to pet stores, elementary schools and day care centers.

Create a website to sell your products if you're willing to ship them.

Pitfalls to Avoid

Some ants bite so be careful in the types you select for your home. Never use imported fire ants.

You cannot ship live ants internationally (too many laws). You can ship within U.S., except to Hawaii, provided you have permits from the US Department of Agriculture (see Resources). Spend time at the USDA Animal and Plant Health Inspection Service website to learn the rules regarding shipment of live insects.

Growth Potential & Expansion

Sell replacement ants and products to ant hobbyists. There aren't a lot of stores or websites that sell ants.

ANT COLONY

Write a booklet or book or create a DVD or video on how to make ant homes and care for them. This is probably better than actually selling live ants considering how many rules and regulations apply to live insect sales.

Competition

Uncle Milton is a favorite of school children and ships, they say, about 30,000 ant farms a month. You need to offer a different environment; e.g., a version of Buckingham Place.

Keys to Success

Learn how to take care of the ants and provide a list of care tips to each customer.

Resources

The father of ant farms is Uncle Milton at
http://www.unclemilton.com/

Ant Colony Developers Association
http://www.antcolony.org/

Buy ants from Life Studies
http://www.antsalive.com
490 S. 400 W.
Hurricane, UT 84737
E-mail: life@infowest.com

U.S. Government website:
USDA Animal and Plant Health Inspection Service
http://www.aphis.usda.gov/

7 Aquarium Maintenance

General Concept

You can always make money doing the things people hate to do. This includes cleaning algae covered aquariums and fish tanks in homes and offices.

Profit Potential

Charge by the hour or by the gallon. For instance, a 20-gallon tank is $20 to clean. Have a minimum fee (say $20) for small tanks. Make sure your fee is high enough to cover your transportation costs. Limit the zip code areas you service so you don't spend all your time in transit.

Equipment Needed

Rubber gloves, algae scraper/pads, plastic razor blade, bleach, water siphon, buckets, lime remover, glass cleaner, filter brush and cleaning agent, gravel vacuum, paper and cloth towels. Never use ammonia products, which kill fish. Buy aquarium safe cleansers and supplies from pet stores. $200 should cover it.

Dependable vehicle to get to jobs and hold your supplies.

Getting Started

If you're not an experienced owner, read up on how to clean an aquarium. You empty all the water, don a pair of rubber gloves, scrub and scrape and clean the tank, then refill it with water and put the fish back. But doing it in the right order is VERY important.

Aquarium Maintenance

This business requires you to know what you're doing. If you're a beginner, buy some used aquariums for practice. Fish are truly delicate creatures.

Advertise in your local newspapers that have a pet section.

Nothing elaborate— "Aquarium Cleaning, We'll do it for you. Call xxx-xxxx." Also place flyers in pet stores and veterinarian offices.

Pitfalls to Avoid

Don't clean or replace all the rocks, plants in the fish tank so the tank's just like new. There's useful bacteria built up in the tank that the fish who've been living there need to remain healthy.

Growth Potential & Expansion

Sell supplies like new filters, plants, fish food, decorations and even fish if you can get a discount from a local wholesaler.

Also consider stocking and renting the aquariums to businesses with active waiting rooms like doctors and dentists.

Competition

Not many people specialize in this.

Keys to Success

Do a good job!

Resources

All the articles you'll ever want to read—scroll to the aquarium business section.

http://www.fishlinkcentral.com
If it relates to fish, it's here.

8 Aromatherapist

General Concept

You use essential oils and scents to maintain or promote good grooming, temperament and health in pets. An example is using essential oils to help rid a dog's coat of fleas or Bach's Rescue Remedy to calm a nervous pet.

You can do this offline in a local market or over the Internet.

Profit Potential

Typical products—shampoos and deodorants in 8-oz bottles—sell for $8 to $14 a bottle. Make your own products for higher profits or sell other supplier's.

Equipment Needed

You must get some training on oils and how to use them prior to starting this business. (See Resources)

You'll need a supply of high quality oils ($100+). Oils can be inhaled, spritzed or dispersed by a diffuser, which may be mechanical, electrical or driven by heat.

I put a couple drops of orange/cinnamon oil in it to send pleasant smells in my living room.

Getting Started

This is a wonderful business for people who already have some training in animal health such as veterinary technicians or groomers.

Aromatherapist

Join the NAHA (see Resources), complete an education program and get certified. You must know which oils are safe to use and which are dangerous for pets.

Once you're ready, make up flyers and leave them with local pet businesses. If you have products to sell (or re-sell), create a website.

Offer your products to veterinarians and animal hospitals. Some are already using scents to help calm excited pets.

Competition

Aromatherapy is very popular in England, Germany and France and gaining acceptance in the U.S. Using it for animals is still relatively new here but that also means the market is wide open.

Pitfalls to Avoid

Don't make claims you can't prove and NEVER claim to cure a disease through aromatherapy. There are many state and federal laws that regulate medical treatments, even for animals. Aromatherapy is not a substitute for veterinary medicine.

Don't use undiluted essential oils directly on pets. They will be too strong and may cause an allergic reaction.

Growth Potential & Expansion

With certification and some experience, you can offer classes to teach pet owners how to use oils for some simple things themselves.

Keys to Success

Using high quality oils. That will give you the best results, which will get you good word of mouth recommendations.

Resources

The National Association for Holistic Aromatherapy (NAHA) (training programs and materials businesses join for $100)
http://www.naha.org/
4509 Interlake Ave N., #233
Seattle, WA 98103-6773
Phone: 206.547.2164

Young Living Essential Oils
(network; i.e., MLM company but supplying high quality oils)
http://www.youngliving.us/
Thanksgiving Point Business Park
3125 Executive Parkway
Lehi, UT 84043

Time Laboratories (high quality oils for sale)
http://www.timelabs.com/
P.O. Box 3243
South Pasadena, CA 91031
E-mail to mail@timelabs.com

Veterinary Aromatherapy
by Nelly Grosjean
(C.W. Daniel Company Ltd, 1994)
available at www.amazon.com for $15.95

Dr. Edward Bach Centre
(a pioneer with renowned products)
http://www.bachcentre.com/
Mount Vernon, Oxfordshire, England

9 ART BROKER

General Concept

You establish a website where artists can show their products, in effect an online art gallery. You can handle the works on a consignment basis, simply charge the artists a periodic fee to show the works or buy and then re-sell the artwork.

You can handle all types of pets or specialize. You can handle any type of artwork or specialize.

Profit Potential

Depends on how you operate your website. Even just operating a gallery and charging for listings can be profitable if you have enough listings. One of the websites in Resources charges $99 a year for one display.

Equipment Needed

You need a computer with shopping cart software that handles photographs well and top quality photo retouching software such as Fireworks, which can enhance and compress the photographs of the artwork. It's vital to have clear photos, but it's also vital to minimize the time it takes to download your site. Few home viewers have high speed access so you must design your website to accommodate access by dial up modems.

Getting Started

As always, pick a name that is clear as to what you are offering rather than something so cute no one can figure out what it means. Pick a name that would match the way a customer would search for your product.

You need inventory to get started. If you're doing consignment sales or just advertising artwork, offer the artists a free, 90-day trial so you can populate your website with enough merchandise. Once you have several artworks on display, you can find paying advertisers or clients. You can find artists at street malls and craft fairs. You can contact local art schools and colleges with art programs.

Once you get started, artists will be telling their friends about your website. Just make sure you only offer products that meet your quality standards.

To find customers, leave flyers at pet related businesses and arts and crafts stores. Try small classified ads in the local newspaper or weekly shopper.

Most importantly, you must get high rankings in the Internet search engines.

Pitfalls to Avoid

Establish polices and stick to them on payment terms, refunds, exclusive listings and types of items you'll handle.

Growth Potential & Expansion

Add classified ads to your website.

Competition

There are not many websites that specialize in pet related art.

Keys to Success

Your graphics must be high quality.

Art Broker

On the other hand, you need a variety of artwork to become successful. Don't reject artwork simply because it doesn't appeal to you. The artistic standard you should use is whether it will sell or not.

Resources

Examples of art gallery sites:

Mutt Art
http://www.muttart.com/

Art Brokerage
http://www.artbrokerage.com/

Sell Your Art Online has an excellent article on how to protect your images from being copied and a sample letter to send a copyright violator
http://1x.com/advisor/security.htm

Example of shopping cart software:
Shop Factory e-commerce

PayPal has a free shopping cart software with credit card processing. You have the option of allowing PayPal to accept credit cards from non-members or restricting credit card purchases to PayPal members only.

http://www.paypal.com

10 BED AND BREAKFAST

General Concept

You no longer have to worry about finding a hotel that will allow pets—you now run one yourself. Operating a Bed & Breakfast is a dream of many people's, but the reality is you have to be prepared to do everything yourself (from fixing leaky faucets to cooking scrambled eggs), and you're on duty 24/7. Regardless, many couples love this business and couldn't image a better lifestyle.

Profit Potential

It's difficult to be profitable with fewer than six rooms (per Professional Association of Innkeepers) although if you live in a popular area that serves tourists year-round, you may make money. The Innkeepers group also stated that the average income of a B&B ranges from $40,000 to $140,000 depending on number of bedrooms.

You can do this on a part-time or seasonal basis if you just want some additional income. Best of all, everything you spend improving your home is usually tax deductible as a business expense.

Equipment Needed

A lovely home with amenities that appeal to tourists. You'll need adequate insurance for property and liability coverage. At some point, a guest will fall down or a child will flood a bathroom.

Your start-up costs vary depending on whether you're acquiring a home and property or renovating an existing B&B. This is not a business that can be opened or operated on a shoestring. Take advantage of resources from the Innkeepers association (see Resources) to help draft a budget.

Getting Started

Get listed in the publications and websites that list B&Bs that allow pets. For example, http://www.doggonefun.com is a popular website for people traveling with dogs. Search Google for other pet-friendly travel sites.

Don't be shy about sending a flyer, e-mail or letter to publications. They need your listing as much as you need to get listed.

Send out press releases to local news media and join national and any state innkeepers association to participate in marketing campaigns. Also join your local Chamber of Commerce.

Create a website for your inn and provide information how to reserve a room online. Many busy people rely on the Internet to plan their vacations.

Growth Potential & Expansion

If you grow weary of running a full-time B&B, you can offer your services to other B&B owners who want to take a vacation but don't have staff to leave in charge of the inn. I know a couple who spend several months a year in the nicest locations imaginable doing this. You must have experience running a B&B, and you must be licensed, insured and bonded.

Once you develop a good reputation, you won't have any problem getting bookings.

If your state doesn't have a state association of innkeepers, start one or offer seminars for other people who want to start a Bed & Breakfast. You'll be surprised how many people that is.

Competition

Check you area and try staying at one or two inns yourself to see how you can distinguish your inn from the others. There may not be many inns in your area that allow pets.

Keys to Success

Stamina and attention to detail are essential. You must have superb people skills and be comfortable around strange pets. A sense of humor is vital—you're going to need it.

The most important key to success, however, is excellent business skill. This is a business that attracts romantics, but it's more important to understand bookkeeping and marketing rather than interior design if you want to stay in business.

Bed and Breakfast

Resources

Professional Association of Innkeepers International
(PAII – highly recommended
membership is $179 but worth it.)
P.O. Box 90710
Santa Barbara, CA 93190
Phone: 805.569.1853

Internal Revenue Service (IRS)
"Audit Technique Guide for Bed & Breakfasts" (a must read)
at
http://www.irs.gov/pub/irs-mssp/b&b.pdf

How To Open and Operate a Bed & Breakfast
by Jan Stankus
(Globe Pequot Press, 5th edition, 1997, 336-pages)
available at www.amazon.com for $14.97

11 BEEKEEPER

General Concept

Another business for rural residents. You raise bees in your backyard and sell beeswax, beeswax candles and/or honey. You probably won't top Burt's Bees for products, but you may supplement your income with local sales at fairs and craft malls. Just don't expect to get rich with this one.

Also, no matter how careful you are, you will at some point get stung.

Profit Potential

Beeswax candles can sell from $1 for a very small one to $30 for one in a clever shape. A bar of honey soap may sell for $5 while a one-pound jar of honey also sells for $5. Pricing of other products such as soaps and furniture polish varies greatly depending on your area and your marketing prowess.

Spend time at the American Beekeeping Federation website (see Resources) for examples of products and pricing.

Equipment Needed

You must live in or create a climate suitable for beekeeping. Bees can't live in extreme cold or heat and prefer temperatures at least in the 50s.

Budget $500 for one hive of bees, hive boxes (called Supers) and equipment to take care of the bees (veil, gloves, smoker, feeding equipment). An extractor to separate combs from honey will be about $1,000. You can easily spend thousands of dollars on equipment so start small. Usually hive boxes come in kits that require assembly.

If you're not a handyman, have someone available to help you get set up.

Getting Started

Do your homework. Learn as much as you can and visit any nearby US Department of Agriculture Extension Service for free and inexpensive information. Join the American Beekeeping Federation (see Resources). Order bees for spring delivery and have them insured for shipment. The bees should be delivered after the date of the last hard freeze for your region. You should be ready to harvest honey within the first year.

Pitfalls to Avoid

Mites are the biggest threat to the bees and have wiped out thousands of honeybee colonies.

Be sure you are not violating any zoning laws by setting up a hive and in many states, you must register as a beekeeper (yes, really) and be subject to periodic inspections.

Competition

This is a small industry, which has been harmed by imported honey; however, the herbal and organic products market continues to expand.

Growth Potential & Expansion

In addition to honey and beeswax, you can collect and sell bee pollen, royal jelly or bee venom.

Once you have several hives, you may offer tours of your beekeeping business to school groups and sell supplies to would-be hobbyists. Offer classes and even make a DVD or video on getting started in beekeeping. In addition to bee hobbyists, target gardeners and wine makers who need bees (or at least bee pollen).

Keys to Success

Keep your bees mite-free and continue learning as much as possible about the business.

BEEKEEPER

Resources

American Beekeeping Federation
(membership fees range from $35 to $250)
http://www.abfnet.org/
P.O.
Box 1337
Jesup, GA 31598-1038
Phone: 912.427.4233

Beekeeping for Dummies by Howland Blackiston
(excellent beginners guide) (For Dummies, 2002, 336-pages)
available for $13.99 at www.amazon.com

Bee supplies:
Dadant and Son's
51 S. 2nd Street
Hamilton, IL 62341

Dadant also publishes the *American Bee Journal*
($21.95 subscription), which is highly recommended.

Western Bee Supplies
http://www.westernbee.com/
P.O. Box 190, 9th & Main
Polson, MT 59860

12   Bird Day Care

General Concept

If local ordinances and zoning allow it, offer to sit pet-birds in your home. This is ideal for people who already love birds and understand how to care for them.

Clients drop their bird off on the way to work or vacation and pick them up later. Few bird lovers want to leave their pets at a day care for dogs or cats!

Profit Potential

Charges typically start at $15 to $20 a day. Extra fees may be charged for cleaning a bird or its cage.

Equipment Needed

Birdcages with feeder drawers that slide out easily. Although many clients may bring the bird in its own cage, some cages are so heavy this isn't feasible. Have covers to put on the cages at night.

Buy good quality bird feed. (Have clients provide special-diet feed and medications.)

Have a pair of gloves (sheepskin mitts sold in auto supply stores are good or heavy leather gloves) if you must handle a bird that seems difficult or aggressive.

Have a couple of bird toys including a feather but ask clients to bring one of the bird's favorite toys with them.

Bird Day Care

Getting Started

Make sure your home insurance covers you for this business. You may need a rider to your existing policy or a new policy.

Distribute flyers, business cards or brochures at vets, pet stores, and local Audubon Societies.

Pitfalls to Avoid

Have clients sign a standard pet sitting type contract. Pet Sitters International sells templates. Make sure you understand whether the client wants the bird let out of the cage or not and whether the client wants you to handle the bird or not. Many clients do not want anyone else trying to hold their birds. My recommendation—don't take the bird out of the cage unless you are an experienced handler.

Make sure the contract authorizes you to take the bird to a vet in the event of an emergency or sudden illness.

Given the small size and weight of a bird, any problem including a loss of blood can quickly become life threatening. Birds are more complex to care for than dogs or cats. Do not attempt this business unless you have experience or are willing to spend the time to learn how to care for birds.

Do not keep birds in a room where other animals have been. Birds are very susceptible to viral and bacterial infections. If you've had Fido or Fluffy in your house, sterilize an area where you can house the birds.

Growth Potential & Expansion

Sell supplies including high-end bird cages and mobile carrying cases.

Competition

Minimal. Most pet day care is aimed at dogs.

Keys to Success

Referrals and testimonials from satisfied clients.

Don't overextend yourself with too many birds and insist on evidence that the birds were recently cleared by a veterinarian to be in a group setting. You don't want a sick bird infecting your other clients.

Sterilize constantly. That includes any toys, equipment and cages that you use for your clients.

Resources

For an example of this business, visit Feathered Playpen
http://featheredplaypen.com/Boarding.html

Birds n Ways, a website all about pet and exotic birds
http://www.birdsnways.com

Guide to a Well-Behaved Parrot (highly recommended) by Mattie Sue Athan
(Barrons Educational Series; 2nd edition , 1999, 144-pages) available at www.amazon.com for $9.56

13 BIRDING GUIDES

General Concept

You create a guidebook describing commercial birding tours. This can be limited to one geographical area (a state or region), the entire U.S. or foreign countries. Reportedly some 70 million Americans have taken up birding as a hobby and with the Baby Boomers aging rapidly, more are likely to follow.

Profit Potential

You make money three ways: 1) selling your guidebook; 2) selling advertising in your guidebook and 3) getting a commission from people who book a guided tour after finding it in your guidebook.

Equipment Needed

Computer with Microsoft Word and an Internet connection. You'll spend a good deal of time using search engines to find these specialized tours.

Getting Started

Pick up copies of bird magazines at Barnes & Noble and search the ads for tour companies.

Also visit any local bird stores such as Wild Birds Unlimited (a national franchise) and ask the managers/owners about tours. Make friends with these people so you can leave your guidebooks there on consignment If you're not already a member of a local Audubon Society or American Birding Association, now is the time to join. Frequent all the birding group meetings you can and ask members what tours they've been on and which ones they liked.

Once you have a list of commercial tour companies, send them individually addressed letters explaining your concept and ask if they offer commissions for customers. For the ones who are interested in being in your guidebook, ask them for information and photos (if you're going to include them) that you can use in the book.

You're unlikely to find a publisher for such a guidebook but this is ideal for self-publishing or print-on-demand (see Resources).

Pitfalls to Avoid

Offer a pre-publication discount so you can get a feel for how many people might buy your book. Leave flyers about your upcoming guide at the bird stores, bird and nature clubs. Don't print too many copies before you know you have a winner.

Avoid do-it-yourselfers who might buy your guidebook but would never take a commercial tour. These are the people who buy the Field guides.

Growth Potential & Expansion

Revise the book periodically and offer it as an e-book. You might even try your hand at leading a tour.

Remember, you don't have to sell millions of copies to make money.

A market with 25,000 people can be very profitable if you are providing targeted information that they can't readily get elsewhere.

BIRDING GUIDES

Competition

This is a pretty open specialty. Most other guidebooks are for do-it-yourselfers and describe areas rather than tours.

Keys to Success

Marketing everywhere and all the time.

Resources

American Birding Association
http://www.americanbirding.org/
P.O. Box 6599
Colorado Springs, CO 80934
Phone: 719.578.9703

http://www.audubon.org/
700 Broadway
New York, NY 10003
Phone: 212.979.3000

Examples of bird tours:
Sarus Bird Tours (a British company specializing in East Africa)
http://www.sarusbirdtours.co.uk/

14 Blacksmith or Farrier

General Concept

You can practice the craft of horseshoeing—still an in-demand service—or make products for the growing number of hobbyists who have taken up this craft.

Although often used interchangeably, a blacksmith is one who makes and repairs things made of iron or steel while a farrier is one who shoes horses, mules, donkeys and occasionally oxen and may or may not be skilled in the iron work done by the blacksmith.

Profit Potential

The Department of Agriculture has estimated there are nearly 10-million horses in the United States today and horses need re-shoeing about every 6-9 weeks. For horseshoeing itself, rates typically are $8-$26 for straightforward shoeing and $35-$75 for handmade shoes. The more complex or custom the job, the more you charge even beyond $75.

You also can make money by making products such as videos, DVDs, reports for the hobby blacksmith. Find someone who is skilled at this and do a joint venture with him or her. You do the production; they provide the performance.

Equipment Needed

Blacksmiths typically use mild steel and wrought iron. The forge is the furnace where metal is heated, and it may be powered by coke, coal, oil or gas. Metal is shaped using a hammer and other tools and wrought into shape on an anvil.

Blacksmith or Farrier

Once you've taken one or two courses and know what types of equipment you want to use (there's also cold shoeing), you can buy what you need. You may even decide to make your own tools.

Getting Started

You need some classroom training. At least 13 states have schools offering programs in horseshoeing. Cornell University has a 16-week program with tuition of $4,500 while Oklahoma Horseshoeing School offers a two-week program for $1,200. Blacksmiths and farriers work in extremes of temperature, ranging from the heat of the forge to freezing conditions outside. When you're ready for business, leave flyers at stables, horse shows, feed stores and equine professional practices.

Pitfalls to Avoid

This is not a business for a 98-pound weakling.

You should be physically fit and able to lift 75-pounds.

Growth Potential & Expansion

If you enjoy iron working and have your own forge or fire pit, you can expand the iron products you make to include candleholders, fireplace tool sets and old-fashioned hand-made iron tools or ornaments. Sell your products at craft fairs and museum stores.

Many people collect antique anvils.

If you find any really old tools, try selling them on eBay.

Competition

This is an in-demand career for those who do it and a growing hobby for those who want to sell products for the blacksmith.

101 Home based Businesses for Pet Lovers

Keys to Success

No matter which path you take—doing the work or writing about it—your skills must be excellent and you must stay current with the trends in blacksmithing.

Resources

American Farriers Organization
(membership is $105; has state chapters)
http://www.americanfarriers.org/
4059 Iron Works Pkwy, Suite 1
Lexington, KY 40511
Phone: 859.233.7411

Farrier Industry Association
(suppliers of products for farriers)
http://www.farrierindustry.org/
403 Axminister Dr.
Fenton, MO 63026
Phone: 636.326.1500

Blacksmith's Journal ($37 annual subscription)
http://www.blacksmithsjournal.com/
Hoffmann Publications, Inc.
P.O. Box 1699 - Washington, MO 63090

15 BREED FISH

General Concept

If you have an aquarium of your own and have suffered sticker shock at the price for rarer species of fish, you've probably considered trying to breed your own fish and sell them. Except for the large, commercial wholesaler, this is rarely a major moneymaker, but with careful selection, you may be able to pay for your own hobby.

Profit Potential

Depends on your fish and its popularity in your area. Small fish may sell for $3-10 while breeding pairs sell for $100 to $250. That's the retail price.

If you sell to local pet shops, they won't want to pay more than 50-cents to $1.50 per fish.

Equipment Needed

At least one breeding pair of fish. An aquarium geared toward the type of fish you want. It may be freshwater or saltwater. Livebearers or egg layers. You need to decide what you want to breed. Consider rare catfish, African cichlids, and marine fish rather than the more common angels, guppies and cory cats.

You'll need food suitable for the fish you're breeding, aquarium cleaning supplies and water. The latter seems obvious but local water varies a great deal and depending on the type of fish you want, you may have to filter or replace your tap water with something more expensive.

Get baggies and rubber bands to take your sold fish to the store or retail buyer.

Getting Started

Unless you already have a market in mind; e.g., members of hobby group, you should survey your nearby pet stores who sell fish and ask them what types of fish they would be willing to buy. You may be surprised.

Explain to all potential customers that your fish are less stressed than fish that have been shipped and must be acclimated to local water conditions.

If you want to sell directly to individuals, advertise in your local free-classified ads newspaper or large Sunday newspaper. Leave flyers at supermarket bulletin boards and send to any fish-hobby groups in your state.

Pitfalls to Avoid

For your breeding pair(s), it's usually safer to buy locally than order through the mail. Shipping is hard on any live animal and the water in your area may not be the idea medium for fish born and bred in another area.

Don't breed a fish that no one wants to buy. Fish, as with other hobbies, go in and out of fashion. One year saltwater aquariums are the rage, the next year they're old hat. Even with that, you may have a batch of fish that the store doesn't want AT THAT TIME.

Offer a guarantee but make it quick, something like 48-hours. Insist your customer return the dead or diseased fish before you replace it or refund the purchase price.

Breed Fish

Growth Potential & Expansion

Sell to hobbyists directly. Be sure to charge enough for shipping. Sending live animals through the mail or delivery service can cost $30 to $60 for domestic deliveries. Don't accept personal checks.

Competition

There are large, commercial fish farms. Your market has to be the rarer species that pet shops have trouble getting or the individual hobbyist who wants personal and fast service.

Keys to Success

Keep the quality of your water (in terms of cleanliness and water chemistry) in the aquarium high. Learn how to efficiently provide constant water and clean the tanks. Over time, you'll also learn what types of fish food work best with your water and fish.

Breed as many fish as possible. Your costs for aquariums, etc are sunk so the more fish you can safely add to your fish farm, the greater your profits.

Make friends with pet shop managers and owners. They can make you a good part-time income if you pay attention to what they want.

Resources

Stuart Chale's fish room (an example of a serious breeder)
http://www.angelsonly.com/hatchery.htm

Aquarium Professionals Group
http://www.aquariumpros.com
2533 Hartrey Ave
Evanston, IL 60201

16 BUILD DESIGNER DOG HOUSES

General Concept

Many people love their dogs but want to keep them outside or at least outside during the day.

If you're a handy man or woman, you can make custom-sized and designed doghouses for your local market and the Internet.

Profit Potential

A man in my area makes dog log houses (like miniature log cabins) and charges $250 for the smallest size. If he delivers and installs it, it's another $75. If you do a custom design, you can charge even more. Two of my favorites are a man who will duplicate the owner's house and another that sells English thatched-cottage doghouses.

Equipment Needed

Do you already have wood working tools such as saw, rulers, levels, etc? If not, you'll need $200-$500 worth of equipment. Then you must decide on materials for your doghouses. You can specialize such as the man who does log cabins or offer houses in a range of materials from wood to concrete to plastic. The design you select will dictate how much material you need.

Getting Started

This is for high rollers so forget the grocery store bulletin boards and try to leave brochures at veterinary offices and doggy day cares. Most pet stores sell mass-produced doghouses so they may not let you leave flyers or brochures there.

Build Designer Dog Houses

If you're near an upscale housing development, leave flyers at the homes that appear to have dogs. If the upscale neighborhood has a local newspaper, see if you can afford to have a flyer inserted in newspaper or a classified ad. This can be surprisingly affordable and reach just about all the homes in a nice area.

Offer a standard product or provide a free estimate of a custom design.

Pitfalls to Avoid

Don't develop a price until you've costed all your materials and your labor. Find a design and build a doghouse for a dog and keep track of what you spend and how long it takes you. It's too easy to underestimate how much you have to charge for a product like this to make it worthwhile to do. Remember, your time is worth something!

Growth Potential & Expansion

In addition to making your own doghouses, you could become a dealer for other companies and even develop a specialized website offering nothing but doghouses. Offer things that no one else has such as air-conditioned doghouses for the Sunbelt owners.

Competition

Not many people specialize in this. Always advertise as "designer" doghouses, which lets people know right away that this is not a discount product. Advertise as Canine Condos by John Doe or Fido Estates or some other catchy name that indicates you have an upscale product.

Keys to Success

Safety first. If you're inexperienced in woodworking or construction, buy commercial plans to ensure you make a safe home. Having a dog house roof collapse on Fido during a heavy rain will not win you any good word-of-mouth and may even generate a lawsuit. Don't make the house a lightning rod and don't use paint or materials that could be harmful to dogs.

Keep the floor of the doghouse off the ground to keep moisture and cold out. Make the house large enough so the dog can turn around and have an elevated bed inside but small and secure enough to keep drafts out.

Resources

For plans:

Radix, Inc.
P.O. Box 948
Ladson, SC 29456-0948
http://www.radixinc.com/dogs/dogs.html

How Mike Did It at
http://www.mikestrong.com/doghouse/
Mikes' step-by-step experience and photos
of many custom doghouses.

For ideas:
McGhee & Co (Thatched Tudor Dog Kennels)
P.O. Box 39
Crozet, VA 22932-0039
Phone: 1.888.842.8241
http://www.thatching.com/dg.html

LaPetite Maison Playhouse, Inc.
(the name says it all)
http://www.lapetitemaison.com/dh.html
Phone: 1.877.404.1184 or lapetitemaison@email.com

17 Build Macquariums

General Concept

You take a page from Macintosh user Andy Ihnatko and make aquariums from discarded Macs. People, especially children, enjoy seeing live fish swim inside a computer monitor.

Profit Potential

One website sells the classic Macquarium for $149.99 (no fish) while another selling the iMac charges $299.95. Do-it-yourself kits usually retail for around $100.

Equipment Needed

You need an empty Macintosh or iMac shell. Try eBay and local computer stores as well as schools that are upgrading computer equipment. Remember, you don't need working computers so you should be able to get them free or very inexpensively. You just need a window on the monitor.

The best fish for these are goldfish. You'll also need thermometer, heater and water pump (total $200) if you want to use any fish more exotic than goldfish.

Getting Started

Visit one or more of the websites in Resources that describe how to make these. Try one or two before you start your business. It helps if you know something about fish—the "computer" part is easier.

Take a photo of the Macquairum and put in on flyers that you distribute at pet stores that carry fish.

Send out news releases (with photo) to your local newspapers and radio/TV.

Pitfalls to Avoid

Someone at some point may obtain a patent on these aquariums and this business may dry up (no pun intended). If you're clever, you'll simply move on to using another type of novelty product to create aquariums.

Do not overcrowd the fish because the water supply is so limited. Two hearty fantail goldfish are the ideal number of occupants.

Remind anyone who buys these that the fish require care just as they would in any aquarium. Sometimes people lose site of the fact that they are buying living things—this is not just a computer simulation! It's a good idea to provide a one-page tip sheet on how to care for the goldfish. If someone wants more exotic fish, let the customer provide them himself.

Growth Potential & Expansion

Create custom Macquariums using a client's own discarded Macintosh and the fish they've selected for the aquarium.

Create videos or DVDs or seminars to teach people how to build these themselves. You might even sell kits with all the equipment needed (including an old Mac) to make one.

This is an ideal add-on to an aquarium maintenance or leasing business as a high-priced, novelty item. You don't have to be limited to the Macintosh. Look around you for other novelty items to serve as aquariums.

101 Home based Businesses for Pet Lovers

If fish aren't you thing, you could create a terrarium for lizards, turtles, spiders, hermit crabs or some other small animal. Remember, don't crowd them as the Mac doesn't have a lot of space for airflow.

Competition

There are websites doing this but probably not much competition in any one local area.

Keys to Success

Your creativity and marketing make you succeed or fail.

Resources

Original instructions:
http://website.lineone.net/ damian.coombes/macplus.pdf

Matt's Macquarium page (his experiences building one)
http://www.iwbyte.com/matt/macquarium.html

Photo gallery of Macquariums (must see site)
http://www.theapplecollection.com/Collection/Macquarium/

Cathy's website (highly recommended)
http://www.amherst.edu/ camiller/macquarium.html

Note: some of these websites are run by college students. If they are no longer operational when you try them, do a search on Google and you'll find plenty of resources.

18 Canine Rehabilitation

General Concept

You help Fido get back on his feet after surgery, injury or illness. This field is only a couple of years old but is expected to grow rapidly in the next few years. Veterinary science now offers as sophisticated (and expensive) treatments for dogs as medical science does for humans.

Given that dogs are living longer but still suffering from genetic disorders and injuries, there will be increased demand for certified canine rehabilitation therapists.

This field requires specialized training and physical stamina; however, it is tremendously rewarding to help a dog regain his ability to walk.

Profit Potential

One couple set up a canine swimming pool and exercise room in their home. Clients bring their dogs to them and the couple charges $35 for one treatment a week or $50 for two treatments a week. They see 40 to 60 dogs a week.

If you visit the animal, the fee generally ranges from $50 to $125 per session, and you need to have some equipment such as balance boards, oversized balls or mini-trampoline.

Equipment Needed

If you're not already a veterinary technician, physical therapist or other health care professional, you'll need up to two years of specialized classes. There are six (as of this writing) veterinary colleges that offer programs but only the University of Tennessee is offering certifications. That is expected to change so check with your state's veterinary college if you want to pursue this but do expect to spend several thousand dollars to get the training you need.

Also, check with your state to see if canine physical therapy requires any special licenses, similar to human physical therapists.

Getting Started

Send flyers to breeders, trainers, veterinarians and animal hospitals. It would be best if you team with an animal hospital or several veterinarians in your area to get referrals.

As this is so new, expect difficulty in getting those first few clients. Once you demonstrate how effective you can be, you can expect word of mouth to grow your business.

After you've treated a few dogs, develop a press release describing one or two success stories and send it to all the local print and electronic news media.

Pitfalls to Avoid

Ensure you have sufficient liability insurance to cover your practice and if you use your home to treat animals, make sure you are not violating any local zoning rules. When you do put a dog in a swimming pool, make sure he's always wearing a life jacket (yes, there are ones for dogs) and the chlorine in the pool is not too strong. Expect to clean pounds of dog hair from the filters after each use!

If you travel to your clients, don't cover too wide an area or you'll spend too much time and money in driving.

Growth Potential & Expansion

Sell products for other practitioners. For instance, many therapists love underwater canine treadmills, but they sell for $14,500 to $50,000 each.

Currently, one company makes them and has sold 53 in four years.

As more people accept how valuable this service can be, there will be a market for effective, simple products that owners can use to treat their dogs themselves.

Competition

Almost none.

Keys to Success

Training and certification; however, a certification in canine rehabilitation may not be as vital if you already are a health care professional certified in a related field.

Not all dogs respond to hydrotherapy so you must be able to offer a range of services.

Resources

Example of a program:
The University of Tennessee (provides courses across U.S.)
http://www.utc.edu/Canine/
offers a seven-course program and certification
1534 White Avenue
Knoxville, TN 37996-1526
Phone: 865.974.3181

Animal Rehabilitation Central
(locate services and schools that offer training)
http://arcvet.net/

19 Cat Breeder

General Concept

You may find it difficult to believe anyone would pay for kittens, but they do for popular breeds (today anyway) including Bengal, Abyssinian, Scottish Fold and Chausie.

Profit Potential

I know a breeder of Bengal cats (very popular right now) who charges between $600 and $900 per kitten. The problem is she also spends $9,000 a year on cat litter and food, $5000 on vet fees and $150 a month for umbrella insurance coverage for her 20 cats. I recommend not trying to breed more than one or two queens. You can always expand to a true cattery if that proves successful, and you enjoy breeding.

Equipment Needed

The going rate for a breeding queen is about $1,500 while a stud may set you back $2,500. This is an average, and you could pay more or less.

You will need $100+ worth of equipment including heating pad, disinfectants, enzyme deodorizes, feeding tubes and feeding syringes, kitten formula, litter pans, scale, first aid kit, and kittening box. Any basic book on cat breeding will list the items needed (see Resources).

Your major recurring expenses, however, will be vet bills and CFA registrations as well as marketing efforts.

Getting Started

Join the Cat Fanciers Association (CFA) (see Resources) and enter the CFA Mentor Program.

Read everything you can about breeding cats and take the Red Cross pet first aid class.

Buy a CFA-registered queen of show-quality of the breed you want to specialize in and show her at cat shows for a few months. This will help you learn the details of the breed standard and network with other breeders in your specialty. That will help when your're ready to pay for a stud service or acquire your own breeding stock.

Advertise in cat magazines and on the Internet. Get listed in CFA.

Pitfalls to Avoid

Most states regulate the sale of animals. You must conform to all the laws in your state and locality. Some of them limit the number of animals you can sell from your home in one year and some require you to offer money-back guarantees. Happily, retail pet sales are not yet regulated by federal government agencies.

Although cats are generally hardier than dogs, they do seem to be more susceptible to infectious diseases. Regular vet exams are necessary.

Growth Potential & Expansion

Unlike many businesses, you don't necessarily make more money by breeding more kittens. It can be difficult to find a breeder willing to provide a stud service of sufficient frequency. You might want to acquire a stud of your own but studs are more difficult to keep than queens.

More cats together also can be a problem. Cats tend to be loners and don't always get along in large groups. Disease control becomes a greater problem, and you may have to expand your home to house multiple cats.

Instead of trying to breed more, you might write a book about your breed of cat or sell items related to your breed.

Competition

Depends on your geographical area and breed.

Keys to Success

Charge enough. Depending on your market, it may be very difficult to charge enough to cover all your expenses. It helps if you specialize in a popular but rare breed.

Socialize your kittens well. Don't have more than two cats littering at one time unless you have help from your family or others. Kittens need individual attention.

Always use a written sales agreement. Get samples from CFA.

Resources

The Cat Fanciers' Association, Inc.
http://www.cfainc.org/
P.O. Box 1005
Manasquan, NJ 08736-0805.
Phone: 732.528.9797

Confessions of a Cat Breeder
http://www.confessionsofacatbreeder.com/intro.html
A popular website for novice breeders.

20 Cat Day Care

General Concept

If your local zoning laws permit it, take care of cats in your home. People drop their cats off on the way to work and pick them up at the end of the day. Have the owner bring the pet's food with them to avoid stomach upsets.

You feed them, clean the litter box, and brush them. If you're good at grooming services like nail cutting, offer that as an extra.

Profit Potential

Develop a price for all-day and half-day care. Typical fees are $15 to $25 for a day. Offer weekly and monthly specials to develop long-term clients.

Charge a late fee so owners don't take advantage of you by not showing up until 9 p.m. instead of 6 p.m.

Equipment Needed

Have different types of cat toys (squeaky toys, balls, ropes, etc.) for all tastes. Some cats are very fearful so ask the owner to bring a favorite toy or something with the owner's scent on it.

Getting Started

Liability insurance (plan on at least $200) in case a cat gets hurt or runs away. After that, it's just how much you want to spend on marketing tools. Your city probably limits the number of animals you can have at one time so make sure you know the rules for your area. Get your business license and start handing

Cat Day Care

out flyers or brochures at veterinarian offices, pet stores and condominium/apartment offices.

Include your hours and rates on a bookmark-like insert so you can change your rates later if you need to. People don't like to have to call a stranger to find out how much something is, so don't be coy. This also helps pre-screen clients.

Pitfalls to Avoid

So many cats that you can't give them all individual attention. Don't let them wander further than your backyard to avoid problems with your neighbors.

Many cats do not like leaving their own home so have a short trial run with a cat (a couple hours) to make sure he's going to accept his temporary residence.

Growth Potential & Expansion

This is a nice business because you can do other things at home at the same time. Want to try selling things on eBay? You can do your Internet work while the cats eat, sleep or play among themselves.

Consider adding a web cam for owners who want to watch their cats while they're at work.

Competition

Not a lot for daycares that specialize in cats.

Resources

Examples of this business:
Cat's Nest at http://www.thecatsnest.com/daycare.htm

Country Side Kennel at http://countrysidekennel.com/

21 Cleaning Bird Cages

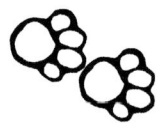

General Concept

Even people who love birds hate cleaning birdcages. You can build a steady business doing this, however, because cages must be cleaned weekly to keep birds healthy. Clean at client's home or have the client drop off the cage at your home.

Profit Potential

Charges typically start at $15 to $25 depending on area of the country.

Equipment Needed

Cleaning supplies. Go natural with Grapefruit Seed Extract (and advertise as using natural products) or baking soda. Commercial products available include Citra-solve or OxyFresh. Also look at the newer steam cleaners although some bird owners are fearful that their heat may release toxic fumes from plastic items in the cages.

Getting Started

Using natural or commercial products shouldn't require more than $100 to get started. Your biggest expense will be marketing materials.

Because you'll travel to client's homes, you'll need dependable transportation and auto insurance that allows you to use your car for business. Distribute flyers, business cards or brochures at vets, pet stores, and local Audubon Societies. Run a small, classified ad in your local free newspaper.

CLEANING BIRD CAGES

Pitfalls to Avoid

If done at client's home, get agreement with the client where the bird remains while his cage is being cleaned.

Make sure the cage is rinsed & dried off thoroughly before putting the bird back.

Don't use harsh chemicals. Never use metal polish on cages, because remaining residue may be toxic to birds. Avoid using bleach on aluminum cages or cage parts, which will discolor aluminum.

Growth Potential & Expansion

Sell supplies including high-end birdcages and mobile carrying cases. Sell replacement parts for cages such as perches.

Competition

Minimal.

Keys to Success

Referrals and testimonials from satisfied clients.

Don't service too large an area. You'll spend too much time and money on gasoline if you drive too much. Target an upscale area.

Resources

Information on birds:
Pet Bird Report at
`http://www.petbirdreport.com`
Birds 'N' Ways at
`http://www.birdsnways.com`

For information on steam cleaning:
`http://www.totalvap.com/`
`http://www.itsagreysworld.com/vap/vaporetto.htm`

22 Computer Pet

General Concept

You make a computer novelty accessory.

The most popular in my area is the computer cat. This is a black silhouette of a cat that this positioned so he is about to jump on or jump off (you position him) the computer monitor.

Any pet or animal—snakes, fish, dogs - that can be positioned on the side or top of a monitor will do. Use Velcro to keep the pet positioned correctly.

Profit Potential

Don't start below $10 each. Take several to a flea market or crafts mall for a couple weeks and offer at different price points each week. See which price and designs works best in your area.

Once you've made these a few times, you can make a dozen (cat size) in an hour. At $10 each, that could be $120 for an hour's work.

Equipment Needed

You'll need a pet silhouette (such as a cat), plywood, jigsaw, Velcro and paint of whatever color you want to use. For example, a black cat is always popular but a Bengal cat might be even more popular. If you don't have a jigsaw but know how to use one, rent one. The rest of the materials are not expensive (less than $100 for all).

If you've never used a jigsaw, take a class at a home improvement store or hire a handyman or handywoman to cut it out for you.

IMPORTANT: When you use the jigsaw, wear protective gear including safety goggles (for eyes) and earplugs.

Getting Started

Create your silhouette (probably about 8-inches long) on card stock. Then cut it out to use as a template.

Place your card on a piece of plywood and trace around the edges with a felt tip marker.

Repeat the shape on the plywood as many times as possible.

Put on your safety equipment and plug in the jigsaw. CAREFULLY cut out the pet shapes.

Paint the shape the color or design you want. When thoroughly dry, varnish or shellac.

Attach a piece of Velcro to its feet, stomach or whatever can be placed on the computer monitor to secure it. It looks best if the pet is simulating a movement such as climbing on top the monitor.

This is a nice weekend business. Spend one night just cutting them out. After that, you can paint and decorate them while you watch TV.

Pitfalls to Avoid

Use the cheapest plywood you can find. Don't be afraid to buy seconds or leftovers. No one will know once the wood is painted.

Be sure to advertise these as "Computer" Dogs or Cats or Snakes or whatever type of pet you make.

Computer Pet

Growth Potential & Expansion

Your market is women. They buy decorative items but sometimes they buy them for the men in their lives, which is why the "computer" theme is important. This expands your potential market.

Create a web page to sell these. If you don't have a merchant credit card account, use PayPal or some other third party credit card merchant.

Joint venture with a pet business related to your type of computer pet. You can offer a package deal, if that makes sense, or have the other businesses just include your flyer with their own marketing.

Competition

Almost none.

Keys to Success

Keep refining your technique and designs. Take your products to plenty of flea market sales and learn what sells the best.

Resources

Home Depot (everywhere in U.S.)
http://www.homedepot.com

Lowe's (almost everywhere in U.S.)
http://www.lowes.com

23 Create Paint-By-Numbers Coloring Book

General Concept

You use a special software program to create a paint-by-numbers coloring book for children using a certain type of pet or multiple types of pets; e.g., cats, fish, snakes or just Labrador retrievers.

Visit the website listed in Resources below to understand how this works and how much fun it is to create.

This is unlikely to be a major moneymaker, but it's a fun sideline for creative types.

You'll delight your own children if you use photos of their pets for the coloring book.

Profit Potential

Rather than trying to sell them one-by-one, visit some local pet businesses and offer to license the artwork pages to them for resale.

The businesses can arrange for the printing or you can do it.

Sell it as a marketing product, not just a coloring book.

Even a license fee of $100 to $500 from four or five businesses is a nice supplement for a small amount of enjoyable effort.

Other businesses that might be interested in doing this are pediatricians, grocery stores and dentist offices or other businesses where children have to wait.

CREATE PAINT-BY-NUMBERS COLORING BOOK

The business could have their company name and contact information on the cover with a title specific for them.

Equipment Needed

You need a scanner or digital camera to capture the images you want to use and a computer.

Most importantly, you'll need a software program that will convert the image into a paint by numbers design.

(See Resources)

Getting Started

Install the software and decide what photographs or drawings you're going to use for the coloring pictures.

Scan the photo or load the graphics file from a disk, choose the brand of paints/crayons to be used and the software will convert your photo to a paint-by-number pattern optimized for the palette you have chosen.

You can print the pattern together with a color key.

When you have enough for a small coloring book (6 to 10 pages), have Kinkos or Office Depot bind them together for you and use it as a sample of what you can do.

Pitfalls to Avoid

Make sure any photos or clip art you use are copyright free or given to you by the copyright holder.

Visit http://www.nolo.com for examples of forms that protect you when you use artwork provided by a third party and licensing agreements.

Growth Potential & Expansion

You'll have to do several to develop your skills.

If you find a design that is popular, you may have it mass-produced and sold widely.

Don't hesitate to try to get on Home Shopping Network at http://www.hsn.com and QVC at http://www.qvc.com as both programs have a constant need for new products to offer and explain at their websites how to submit products for their review.

Competition

You'll probably be the only one in your town doing this.

Keys to Success

Your creativity and marketing make you succeed or fail, but don't expect to get rich.

Resources

Color By Number software program ($19.95)

http://www.stoik.com/hobby/colorbynumber.htm

You can download a free demo.

24 CRITTER PRODUCTS

General Concept

You make products for critters or small animals such as the guinea pig (or more accurately the cavy), chinchilla, degus, ferrets, flying squirrels, gerbil, hamster, hedgehog, rat, or other. These small animals, sometimes called vest pocket pets, are growing in popularity but do not have as many competing products as the more common dogs and cats.

Profit Potential

Deluxe kits (cages plus accessories) often retail for about $50 while two-story cages with accessories retail for $70-80. One deluxe "patio home" sells for $100. Litter kits usually retail for around $20.

Consider selling products designed for cats or small dogs, such as front-type carriers, for critters as well.

Equipment Needed

Most of the rodent pets do not like to play with pure toys; e.g., plush toy. Their idea of play is running free around the house. What they need most are good quality cages with ramps, wheels, balconies, litter pan, feeding pan, water bottle with sipper (not an open dish) and doors on top and bottom for easy accessibility and easy cleaning.

Lightweight, mobile cages with these features would be a blessing for many pet owners. Avoid cages with wire or mesh bottoms as small feet can get stuck easily. A cage with a solid bottom is safer and easiest to clean although wire or mesh sides

101 Home based Businesses for Pet Lovers

or top are fine. Add nontoxic, easy-to-clean bedding and a publication that explains how to care for the pet.

You can make a cage yourself or buy them wholesale and add to it to create a total

"deluxe starter cage for ferret/degus/hamster/etc."

You could also offer litter kits (litter box, litter and booklet on cleaning and dealing with litter).

Getting Started

Get a state re-seller's permit and find a reliable wholesaler or distributor that can provide you with needed supplies in a timely manner.

Visit your local pet shops and see if they handle these types of pets or at least provide supplies for them. The smaller pet shops usually do not have much in the way of critter supplies and may be willing to accept your deluxe starter kits on a consignment basis.

Market to schoolchildren and their parents.

These types of pets are usually chosen by elementary and middle school children. The students study them in a class and then want one for their own. Advertise or publicize your product(s) in publications targeted at students, teachers or families. Most larger cities have such weekly or monthly free publications that accept advertising.

Pitfalls to Avoid

Don't invest too much money in inventory. Create a couple of kits so you can take photos of them for advertising. Otherwise, wait until you get an order and then build the kit. You may even offer kits at two or three price points depending on the quality and luxury the customer wants in the kit.

Growth Potential & Expansion

Expand the deluxe kits you offer by breed. You could start selling the animals as well but there are many local, state and federal laws that regulate sale and handling of rodents. Be sure you understand how to stay legal if you decide to do this.

Toys and clothes for rodents haven't caught on but may be due for a popularity surge. The best product would be an active toy that pet and owner could play together.

If you want to expand your product line, you can add treats such as dandelions or natural foods like carrots or spinach. Make sure the treats have not been treated with chemicals or pesticides. If you can grow or buy organic produce, you may be able to re-sell to rodent owners at substantial profit.

Competition

Your challenge will be getting your product known.

Keys to Success

Offer quality, safe products.

Resources

Animal Network Critter Collection website
(information on all types of critters)
http://www.animalnetwork.com/
critters/profiles/default.asp
They also publish Critters USA magazine and other specialty publications—highly recommended.

Boo and Bears Guinea Pig Boutique, example of a website devoted to the sale of critter products
http://www.jmalms.com/guinea girls HP.htm.

25 CROSS STITCH PATTERNS

General Concept

You create cross-stitch patterns based on photographs of pets sent to you by their owners. If you know how to do cross-stitch and have the right software, this is an easy and fun business to operate.

Profit Potential

Custom patterns typically sell for about $10. You can charge more if you do the cross stitching, but as that is so time consuming, it's better to just create and sell the patterns. Pattern books can retail for as much as $40.

Equipment Needed

You need a computer, a scanner, a color printer and software to create the pattern (see Resources).

Add to your designs with clip art especially geared toward holiday and birthday themes.

Getting Started

Buy the software and try creating a couple of patterns that you then stitch or have a friend do. Make sure you understand how to use the software and create workable patterns.

Offer your product at craft fairs and flea markets. This will help you learn what your customers want or don't want. If you enjoy this, you can rent a permanent space at a local craft mall.

Once you're confident in your skill, run small classified ads in commercial pet publications. Start locally with any pet newspapers or free-classified ad newspapers.

Once you've done a few patterns, try advertising in the wider circulation but more expensive publications such as Cat Fancy or other pet publication.

Remember, everyone goes after the dog and cat market. You might be better off trying horses or reptiles. People love those pets just as much as Fluffy and Fido.

Pitfalls to Avoid

Make certain the patterns you create are workable.

Beware of the Internet. There's a tremendous amount of copyright violations as people share patterns electronically. Many commercial pattern companies have experienced significant drop in income over the past few years.

By offering custom patterns, you avoid the worst of the illegal copying problems. Rather than rely on Internet sales, however, use the Internet as an advertising vehicle for your product but provide patterns only by the U.S. mail.

Growth Potential & Expansion

Create a book of patterns, either with a particular pet or a type of pet such as pattern book devoted to Yorkshire Terriers. This a great Christmas and birthday gift for crafters.

Competition

Not many cross stitch businesses target pet owners with custom patterns.

CROSS STITCH PATTERNS

Keys to Success

Getting your product known to pet owners will be the biggest hurdle.

Resources

Software:
PC Stitch software (less than $50)
http://www.pcstitch.com/

M&R Technologies, Inc.
2445 East River Road - Dayton, OH 45439

Website with free patterns and ideas:
Stitch Alley
http://www.stitchalley.com/

Trade association:
National Craft Association (NCA)
offers merchant credit card accounts
http://craftassoc.com
2012 E. Ridge Rd., #120
Rochester, NY 14622
Phone: 800.715.9594

26 Custom Calendars

General Concept

You use photographs of pets to create a calendar for the owner. See Resources for some ideas on how creative this project can be. People love photos of their pets especially when they're puppies or kittens.

You can have customer provide the photos, take them yourself or get a referral fee from a pet photographer you use for the work.

Profit Potential

Custom calendars, depending on size, usually sell for $20 to $50 each.

Equipment Needed

You need a computer and specialized software to create calendars.

You'll also need a quality photo retouching software such as Jasc Paint Shop Pro (now available at less than $100).

You need a quality laser printer, which will cost several thousand dollars, or you may hire a printer to do that aspect of the job.

Getting Started

Create your work and send out flyers to pet businesses and display your wares at pet shows and competitions. Make a full court press marketing effort beginning in August through mid December.

Offer to create calendars on CD-ROMs and DVDs for customers. Run small classified ad in pet publications targeted to pet owners. You also might try to joint venture with a pet business such as a groomer to offer the calendars at a discount with the groomer's business contact information on each page.

Pitfalls to Avoid

Never use a photograph or drawing if you don't know the source and don't have a release.

Growth Potential & Expansion

Offer calendars in other languages, such as Spanish and advertise in newspapers that cater to foreign population. There are very few companies offering these types of personalized products for foreign-speaking U.S. residents.

Consider affiliate sales of commercial animal calendars through Calendars.com, which is part of Barnes and Noble at http://www.calendars.com/.

It's easy to create an affiliate link if you have a website.

Competition

There are Internet competitors but few local business that do any aggressive marketing.

Keys to Success

You must offer quality products. You've probably seen the cheap-looking calendars you often get from real estate agents and other sales people. Don't go that route. If you can't afford quality full-size calendars, go with small calendars about index-card size that can be pasted on computer monitors and cash registers.

Resources

Make Your Own Chinese Calendar
http://thunder.eeap.cwru.edu/ccal/index.html

Example of website doing this business:
Personal Gift Calendar (nice line of products)
http://www.personalgiftcalendar.com/
P. O. Box 297-276
Brooklyn, N.Y. 11229

Software to make calendars:
Broderbund Calendar Creator 9.0
http://www.broderbund.com
versions range from $30 to $70.

You also can use any desktop publishing software such as Microsoft Publisher or Print Shop although you may want to create your own templates.

If you want, concentrate on marketing and photography and subcontract the actual calendar production:Calendar Creations
http://www.calendarcreations.net/

Also check out local printers and the office supply stores for rates
on printing.

27 Custom Pet Portraits

General Concept

If you're an artist with a love of animals, you can create a custom pet portrait using a color, close-up photo of a pet. Coat the finished surface with a sealant and frame so they can be set on tables or hung on a wall. Also offer paintings on any surface such as marble, rocks, plaques or wood.

Even if you accelerate the process by using a software program, the appearance of a hand painted portrait adds value and allows you to charge a higher price than a mere print.

Profit Potential

Typical price for a standard (5 x 7 inch) portrait is $60 plus shipping and handling.

Charge more for unusual surfaces or large (horses) pets or larger size portraits.

Equipment Needed

Your artist medium of choice—acrylics, charcoal, pencils, etc.

Use artist's canvass or quality 80-lb weight, acid-free paper so it won't yellow over time. Computer with photo enhancing software such as Photoshop, if you're rich or Picture It, if you're not.

Software program such as Corel Painter (about $300), which is the best one currently on the market that can create a portrait-like effect. Note—the software does not turn you into an artist. It just accelerates your work, but if you don't have the talent and training to begin with, you may not be pleased with the results.

Getting Started

Do it the old-fashioned way if you have the talent or use a computer software program to quicken the process.

Do your own pet and then take it to a flea market or crafts fair and see if people are willing to order a portrait.

Pitfalls to Avoid

If you ship a matted and framed product, always insure when you ship. It is too easy to have a portrait damaged even if you pack well. Roll this cost into your shipping price so a customer cannot delete it.

It's less risky to ship an unframed product as glass breaks so easily but still insure the product.

Growth Potential & Expansion

Add a pet photography business or joint venture with one to combine both services into your offering. You can photograph the pet at his home and then create a portrait.

Competition

There's considerable competition thanks to the Internet enabling a portrait to be created from anywhere in the world. You need to distinguish your product and be very, very good to get business.

Concentrate on your local area to start. There's not competition in every city and you may be able to sweep up many commissions in local upscale and active-adult retirement areas.

Custom Pet Portraits

Keys to Success·

You must be better and more creative than the average Sunday painter.

If you travel to your customer be sure to have them reimburse you for travel costs and your time. You can't be creating products when you're driving 300-miles to an appointment.

Resources

How to Draw Lifelike Portraits from Photographs
by Lee Hammond
(North Light Books, 144-pages, 1995)
get it for $17.49 at www.amazon.com

Corel Corporation makes Painter
http://www.corel.com

Painted Snapshot (a must see)
http://www.paintedsnapshot.com

An example of the work from the artist above:
http://www.cassingham.com/painting.html

28 Custom Screen Savers

General Concept

You get photos from customers of their pets and convert them into screen savers or desktop wallpaper for their computers. This is easy to do with the right software but don't expect it to be a cash cow.

Profit Potential

These typically sell for around $20.

Equipment Needed

You need a computer with Internet connection. Have plenty of memory for graphics programs you'll need.

Digital camera if you want to take photographs of local pets. ($300 max)

Software to create screen savers ($100 max) and photo software to reverse, tone and size the image. You can go for a high-end product like Adobe Photoshop but a cheaper product such as Microsoft Picture It will do just fine.

Getting Started

Try creating screen savers using your own pet so you learn how to make them.

Develop a flyer with a photo of a screen saver and then take them around to the pet businesses and professionals in your area. Try to team with a local business, such as a pet groomer, to offer the screen savers either at a discount for their customers

Custom Screen Savers

or as a premium for their customers with their logo and contact information.

Pitfalls to Avoid

Anyone can make screen savers. Target people who are too busy or not technically oriented so that they're willing to pay someone else to do it. Don't expend major efforts with young pet owners or schools where everyone probably does things like this for fun.

Growth Potential & Expansion

Add enhanced capability such as Flash and 3-D effects.

Expand beyond the pet market and sell local businesses or professionals on the idea of creating advertisements or marketing tools through the screen savers that they give to customers.

Competition

Many sites offer screen savers but few target pet owners exclusively.

Keys to Success

Create screen savers for Macs as well as PCs.

Resources

Xemi Computers for software
http://www.xemico.com/groups/ssavers/

Screen Saver Studio software
http://www.screensaverstudio.com/

Make Custom Screen Savers
http://www.customsavers.com/

29 Custom Stuffed Animals

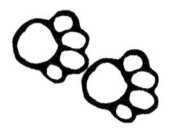

General Concept

This is not a taxidermist! This is a crafts business where you create stuffed animals to look like a beloved pet or a type of pet the customer would like to have but for some reason can't.

This can be a fun business for someone who wants to combine their craft skills with their love of pets and who has a strong artistic sense. It does require strong sewing skills.

People love to get and give stuffed animals, and these make charming gifts for children.

Profit Potential

Typical prices for stuffed animals range from $9 for a hamster to $99 for a St. Bernard.

If you are skilled enough to be able to create a look-alike stuffed animal from a photo or real pet, you can charge more.

On the other hand, you may go for more creative and less lifelike stuffed animals if you have a zany sense of design that appeals to other people.

Equipment Needed

Sewing or embroidery machine, depending on the craft you want. Supplies to make the stuffed animal, again depending on the type you decide to create. Most people start with foam, high quality fabric and the eyes, whiskers, etc that are needed for the specific animal.

Custom Stuffed Animals

Getting Started

Make a couple different designs. Try to sell them at craft fairs, flea markets and eBay. You need to find out what type of designs are most appealing to people.

Alternately, get a resellers certificate from your state and buy some wholesale plush stuffed animals. Customize already made ones with special clothing or added features. Then try to sell them the same way.

Pitfalls to Avoid

Don't charge too little.

This business only works when you customize. You'll never be able to compete on price with retail merchants; you need to create a custom look that justifies your higher price.

Growth Potential & Expansion

Get other people to make them for you and concentrate on marketing. Contract with sales representatives to market your products to other areas of the country.

Once you have a dependable source, you can sell to organizations—service groups, sororities, and clubs—and have the stuffed animals customized with their logo, motto, colors, or whatever unites the group. It's more profitable to sell to a large group rather than rely on single sales to individuals.

Competition

Many stores sell stuffed animals. Few places sell customized stuffed animals or exotic breed stuffed animals.

101 Home based Businesses for Pet Lovers

Keys to Success

Keep up-to-date with latest fads in the crafts market. Revise your marketing and product as needed. If you do this for long, you'll need to add at least one product each year to keep your line fresh. Develop a theme so you can create a product line.

You must be better and more creative than the average home-sewer.

Resources

Handmade for Profit
by Barbara Brabec
(M. Evans and Company, Inc., 372-pages, 2002)
Available at www.amazon.com for $14.95

National Craft Association
http://www.CraftAssoc.com
E. Ridge Rd. #120
Rochester, NY 14622
Phone: 800.715.9594

American Pet Products Manufacturers Association, Inc.
(the trade organization)
http://www.appma.org
255 Glenville Road
Greenwich, CT 06831
Phone: 203.532.0000

For examples of products beyond dogs and cats -
This Place Is a Zoo
http://thisplaceisazoo.com/products/hamster-guinea.html

30 Deliver Kitty Litter

General Concept

You deliver kitty litter to cat owners in upscale and retirement communities. For an additional fee, wash litter boxes and replace with new litter.

Profit Potential

Charge on a weekly or monthly basis. You'll run yourself ragged doing this on an on-demand basis. At least require 24-hours notice before scheduling a delivery and have a minimum fee (usually $15 to $25).

Equipment Needed

Dependable vehicle, pickup truck or van works best, with substantial liability insurance because you're using it for business purposes. Resellers permit from your Secretary of State's office so you can buy litter from wholesalers and not pay a sales tax.

Liability insurance could be thousands of dollars a year depending on where you live. Shop around for rates.

Getting Started

Get your business license and start handing out flyers or brochures at veterinarian offices, active retirement areas (e.g., Del Webb Sun Cities) and condominium/apartment offices.

Be sure all marketing materials state which geographical areas you service (by zip code or name) and include a price schedule. This pre-screens clients and doesn't annoy those who don't want to be bothered having to call to get prices.

Pitfalls to Avoid

Don't service too large a geographic area. You'll waste time traveling and spend too much in vehicle expenses. Go for the upscale, expensive areas.

Growth Potential & Expansion

Sell upscale litter trays and cat condos that you install. This is great for active retirement areas where the cat owner is too busy or doesn't want to fool with heavy, unassembled items.

Take litter boxes with you to clean and sanitize and charge extra for this service.

Competition

Not much.

Although pet food delivery is popular, not many areas offer this specialty. Target upscale senior citizen areas where the pet owners don't want to or can't lug 25-pound litterbags.

Keys to Success

Distribute door hangers in the upscale area(s) you want to service advertising odor free cat litter.

Repackage bags so you aren't leaving a heavy bag with a senior citizen. Five-pound bags will help sell your service.

Resources

Example of a website offering this service:
Pet Food Services
http://www.petfoodservices.com/services.htm

31 Designer Jewelry for Pet and Owner

General Concept

You create and sell matching jewelry for pets, usually dogs but sometimes cats, and their owners. One successful California woman sells sterling silver charm bracelets. The dog's version is a dog collar with silver charms in various bone shapes. The owner's version is a traditional silver charm bracelet with matching bone charms. She also offers seashells and sea creature charms.

Profit Potential

The charm bracelets mentioned above start at $60 and go up to $120 depending on size. Custom designs and more expensive materials draw a higher fee.

Equipment Needed

Depends on your materials. You will need jewelry tools such as crimping pliers, wire, and jump rings. Visit some jewelry stores for ideas and crafts stores for materials. Try making a few designs before you settle on the materials you want to use. For example, you may like beads better than silver or prefer working with crystals. Then find wholesale sources or distributors using the *Thomas Register* or see if the manufacturer's name is on the materials you like to use.

101 Home based Businesses for Pet Lovers

Getting Started

One woman who now nets $100,00 a year started about 10 years ago with her own sterling silver charms. She showed her designs at two jewelry shows a month for six years. She's now in some large department stores, does upscale home shows and sells at larger arts and crafts fairs. She still does the designs but has three women doing the manufacturing.

Once you have some prototypes, you must attend the major pet product shows and larger jewelry or gift trade shows (see http://www.merchandisegroup.com/merchandise/index.jsp for locations). Also send press releases to local media and pet publications. If you use e-mail, you can send a photo of you and your pet wearing matching jewelry.

Pitfalls to Avoid

Include a warning with every item that the pet jewelry should be worn only when someone is present. Never leave the pet alone while he's wearing the jewelry. This is for special occasions only. It would be possible for him to snag a charm on something and harm himself trying to get free.

Growth Potential & Expansion

Add new designs at least twice a year. You can expand pet/owner matching designs in items such as sweaters, rain gear, shoes, and hair accessories. Your imagination is your only limitation.

Competition

There are some competitors selling pet jewelry but few that sell matching items for pet and owner.

Designer Jewelry for Pet and Owner

Keys to Success

Your creativity and relentless marketing.

Develop a signature product or design to anchor your line and be associated only with you. This field is going to expand (I believe) as more Baby Boomers fill their empty nests with their pets and treat Fido and Fluffy like children.

Resources

Jewelry Making for Fun and Profit
by Lynda S. Musante & Maria Given Nerius
(Prima Publishing, 2000, 352-pages)
Buy at www.amazon.com for $13.99.

Examples of websites selling designer jewelry:
The signature piece is pink or white pearls with sterling silver heart-shaped pet ID tag.
The pearls are real and start at $60.
http://www.bijouxfourpawas.com

Dekapets offers a charming line including Hawaiian designs.
http://www.dekapets.com/petjewelry.html

Calling All Dogs sells other people's designs.
http://www.callingalldogs.com/products/instyle/jewelry_for_dogs.htm

32 Dog Cross-Breeder

General Concept

If you love a particular breed of dog and own a purebred, you've probably at some point thought about breeding your dog.

For a one-time family experience, it may be fine to breed Fido. As a business, however, breeding is expensive and risky. If you want to try this as a business, get into the more trendy and growing subset, the crossbred dog.

For instance, one of the most popular crossbreeds is Labradoodles. They have—it is believed—the easy-going, people-oriented temperament of the Labrador retriever and the brains and minimal shedding of the poodle.

Profit Potential

A pet quality puppy sells for around $1000. Remember though that you don't breed puppies every month.

Equipment Needed

In addition to the normal dog equipment (leashes, bowls, etc), you'll need a whelping box (many breeders like to have a light bulb on top), clean towels, sterile scissors, cotton, tincture of merthiolate, baby oil, sterile thread, pencil, scale, alcohol, small cardboard or other box, heating pad, eyedropper and many newspapers. If you're handy, you can make the whelping box yourself. Equipment is not expensive, at most a couple of hundred dollars if you buy everything new.

Dog Cross-Breeder

What is expensive are the vet bills and genetic testing (approximately $100 per test). How many and what kind of tests depend on your dog breed and its genetically predispositioned diseases.

Getting Started

Join a breed club. The American Kennel Club website (http://www.akc.org can provide contact information. Visit your library and start reading about breeding and genetic testing. Read, study, read, study. The Resources section has one basic, reader-friendly book to get you started.

Join the breeder's group sponsored by the brand of dog food you want to use. Purina http://www.purina.com/breeders/ and Iams http://www.iams.com both have discounts and samples to breeders who join their groups.

Once you have puppies for sale, advertise at vet offices, groomers, dog shows, your local newspaper Sunday classified in the Pets for Sale section and on your on website.

Pitfalls to Avoid

Most states regulate the sale of animals. You must conform to all the laws in your state and locality. Your zoning may limit the number of dogs you can have in your home.

Vet bills are one of the key costs of this business. Always feed premium quality dog food. This will help reduce common illnesses and appearance problems.

Some states are creating statutory warranties for congenital and hereditary disorders in dogs. Complying with these laws will require you to do genetic testing of your dogs.

Growth Potential & Expansion

If you want to crossbreed, you must be willing to do the research to learn about genetics and how to select the best dogs for breeding. Besides the Labradoodle, other popular cross breeds include Goldendoodle (Golden Retriever-poodle cross) and Schnoodles (Schanuzer-poodle cross). (Notice the theme of getting the poodle's brains and low coat maintenance but without the Type A temperament). Another crossbreed to consider is the American Hairless Terrier, which was developed just for people allergic to dog fur. If you have a purebred, prize-winning male dog, you may be able to offer him for stud service for several hundred dollars. In lieu of payment, you might ask for the pick of the litter puppy and then sell the puppy.

Competition

Not much—yet.

Keys to Success

Learn to give shots yourself and buy your medications from Internet websites such as `http://www.drsfostersmith.com`.

Create a website so customers can find you and get listed in all the search engines.

Resources

Breeding Dogs For Dummies
by Richard G. Beauchamp
(the beginners book)
(For Dummies, 2002, 336-pages)
$15.39 at www.amazon.com

Dog Crossbreeding website
http://www.dogcrossbreeding.com/

33 Dog Day Care

General Concept

If your local zoning laws permit it, take care of dogs in your home. People drop their dogs off on the way to work and pick them up at the end of the day. Have the owner bring the dog's food with them to avoid stomach upsets.

You feed them, take them for walks, brush them and for an extra fee, give them a bath. If you're good at grooming services like nail cutting, offer that as an extra.

Profit Potential

Develop a price for all-day and half-day care. Typical fees are $25 to $30 for a day. Offer weekly and monthly specials to develop long-term clients. Charge a late fee so owners don't take advantage of you by not showing up until 9 p.m. instead of 6 p.m.

Equipment Needed

A ground floor home with a large backyard. Have different types of dogs toys (squeaky toys, balls, ropes, etc.) for all tastes. Also necessary is a pooper-scooper for cleaning your yard and cleaning products for indoor accidents. Recommended is Nature's Miracle.

Liability insurance (plan on at least $200) in case a dog gets hurt or runs away. After that, it's just how much you want to spend on marketing tools. Your city probably limits the number of dogs you can have at one time so make sure you know the rules for your area.

Dog Day Care

Getting Started

Get your business license and start handing out flyers or brochures at veterinarian offices, pet stores and condominium/apartment offices.

Include your hours and rates on a bookmark-like insert so you can change your rates later if you need to. People don't like to have to call a stranger to find out how much something is, so don't be coy. This also helps pre-screen clients.

Pitfalls to Avoid

Don't have so many dogs that you can't give them individual attention. Bored dogs will enrage your neighbors with their barking, digging and soiling.

Interview each dog before accepting him or her to ensure they can play with other dogs and insist on proof of up-to-date vaccinations.

Growth Potential & Expansion

This is a nice business because you can do other things at home at the same time. Want to try selling things on eBay? You can do your Internet work while the dogs eat, sleep or play among themselves.

Offer "doggy play groups" to entice clients who just need to socialize their dogs for a couple hours a day. Also consider adding a web cam for owners who want to watch their dogs while they're at work.

Competition

Lots—but good word of mouth will get you new clients.

101 Home based Businesses for Pet Lovers

Keys to Success

Love the dogs you take care of and be dependable. Take only adult, housebroken dogs or at least limit puppies to one at a time.

Resources

Visit www.dogwise.com for a book and video on how to set up and run a dog daycare.

Sample website:
http://www.anasark.com
for Maryland Doggy Dare Care
American Boarding Kennels Association
http://www.abka.com/
1702 East Pikes Peak Avenue
Colorado Springs, CO 80909
Phone: 719.667.1600

34 Dog Show Handler

General Concept

If you work well with animals and can travel continuously, you might consider becoming a dog handler. The handler is the person that houses, conditions, trains and shows a client's dog (usually dogs although cats also have shows) in professional competitions.

This, however, is another business that is more suited for rural or suburban residents as you need a kennel to keep the dogs.

Profit Potential

There are some 2,500 dog shows across the USA each year with some 300,000 dogs participating! Handlers charge $50 to $100 per ring appearance plus expenses with a bonus if the dog wins a best in breed or show competition. If you make it to Westminster, you might charge $1,000 per ring appearance.

Equipment Needed

A reliable truck or SUV that can take as many dogs as you can handle to your shows. A kennel at home sized to handle as many dogs as you want to have. Grooming equipment and premium dog food. How much this all takes depends on what you have to start with.

Getting Started

Show your own dogs if you have them. Otherwise become a handler's assistant. You need to get known in the dog show world, and it's easier if you find someone to mentor you for a while and if you specialize in a few dog breeds.

If you weren't born into the dog show world, attend as many as you can and volunteer your services even if it's just as an usher. Get to know as many professional handlers and judges as you can. When you find a handler that you like, approach him/her about becoming their assistant.

Pitfalls to Avoid

Don't omit any expenses in calculating your cost. Those will include vet fees, grooming supplies, dog show entry fees, advertising or marketing fees, dog photographs, premium food and appropriate toys. Never let an owner or handler get too far behind in paying their bills. It can be very difficult to collect from wealthy people. Get paid at the beginning of the month for that month. Stop servicing the owner if they become delinquent.

Growth Potential & Expansion

Once the pressure and constant travel get to you, consider becoming a dog show judge.

This is strictly regulated by the American Kennel Club and requires a minimum of 12-years of experience. Visit their website for more information: http://www.akc.org.

Competition

There's considerable competition. Successful handlers make six-figure incomes, and it takes a long time to become well known.

Keys to Success

Become certified by the American Kennel Club (AKC) Registered Handlers Program. This requires seven years of experience

Dog Show Handler

with a maximum of four years as an assistant handler and three years on your own as well as a kennel that meets the AKC standards.

Visit http://www.akc.org/ dic/events/conform/handlersprogram.cfm for more information.

Learn to understand the judges. The world of dog shows is a small one, and you will meet the same judges at many shows. Learn what they like and don't like in the breed they judge. There are fads and fashions in judging dog breeds and dog performances that you must understand.

Learn to handle the owners. Remember the owners have a lot of money and emotional capital tied up in the dog you're handling. You need to calm and soothe upset owners while still exercising enough authority to maintain control of the situation.

101 Home based Businesses for Pet Lovers

Resources

Professional Handlers Association
http://www.infodog.com/misc/pha/phamain.htm
17017 Norbrook Drive
Olney, MD 20832
Phone: 301.924.0089

Dog Handlers Guild
http://www.infodog.com/misc/dhg/dhgmain.htm
413 Dempsey Avenue SW
Buffalo, MN 55313
Phone: 612.682.3366

American Kennel Club Registered Handlers Program
http://www.akc.org/dic/events/conform/handlersprogram.cfm
AKC Headquarters
260 Madison Ave, New York, NY 10016
Phone: 919.816.3884

35 Dog Trainer

General Concept

If you're good with dogs, this is an easy business to enter and one that's always in demand. But remember, you're not just training the dog, you're training the owner so people skills are important.

Profit Potential

Charge by the hour or number of visits, such as six one-hour sessions over six weeks.

Equipment Needed

Your experience and skills plus a few tools like leashes, houseline (long light leash), collars and training tools that you like. Some trainers use clickers; some trainers use prong collars. The best trainers are able to use different tools depending on the dog's temperament.

Have liability insurance in case the dog is injured or injures someone and have health insurance for yourself. Get a tetanus shot prior to starting your business.

Getting Started

Consider specializing in correcting certain, common behaviors such as jumping up, excessive barking, or digging.

If you can apprentice with a trainer you admire, all the better.

Establish relationships with veterinarians, groomers, non-chain pet stores, pet sitters and humane societies. Volunteer to work at shelters to get your name known. Leave marketing materials like business cards everywhere and ask clients for referrals.

See if you can teach a course at your local college or high school and submit articles on common dog issues to your local news media.

Pitfalls to Avoid

Flat fees with a guarantee (e.g., housebreak your dog in three lessons) are not recommended; some dogs are very difficult and some owners unconsciously sabotage training. This is a surprisingly political area with some people adamant about positive training and clickers and others who rely on the traditional methods such as slip collars. Don't waste time in fruitless arguments.

Growth Potential & Expansion

Sell supplies and pet food.

Competition

Depends on your area. This is a hot occupation.

Keys to Success

Great word of mouth and referrals from clients.

Understanding dog temperaments—some dogs are Lassies; some dogs are Cujos.

Most important—train the owners. The dog will never be a successful graduate unless you are able to control and guide the owners in how to care for the dog. Many people are good with animals but not with people. Don't make the mistake of thinking you can be a success in this business if you can't deal with people.

DOG TRAINER

Resources

National Association of Dog Obedience Instructors
http://www.nadoi.org
729 Grapevine Hwy. #369,
Hurst, TX 76054-2085

Association of Pet Dog Trainers
http://www.apdt.com
P.O. Box 385
Davis, CA 95617

Dog Problems
by Carol Lea Benjamin.
A guide for dealing with typical dog problems.
(Howell Book House, 2nd ed, 1989, 224-pages)
Available at www.amazon.com for $10.47

36 Dog Walker

General Concept

You give Fido his daily walk or walk(s). This service can be combined with a pet sitting service or offered by itself. Some people in large cities do nothing but walk dogs all day long. Think of the great exercise they're getting.

Profit Potential

Depending on your area, charge $10 to $25 for a 30-minute walk. One woman in a large city walks 80 dogs a week. Another in New York City charges $15 for a half-hour walk.

This is unlikely to be a full-time income but a few thousand dollars a year and plenty of fresh air may be just what you're looking for.

Equipment Needed

Get one or two leashes to have on hand. You'll need a pooper-scooper or baggies to pick up his poop and a spray bottle with paper towels for other accidents.

It's a good idea to have pepper spray or squeeze bottle with vinegar in case a stray dog attacks you. If you have a backpack or fanny pack, carry a small first-aid kit. Accidents happen suddenly in parks and wooded areas, and you may be some distance from a veterinary office.

All the equipment you'll need should set you back less than $200.

Dog Walker

Getting Started

Join one of the pet sitting organizations (see Resources) so you can get their group rate on liability insurance. This may seem like an unneeded expense until you have a dog that knocks down an elderly passerby who breaks her hip. Don't take chances with your financial future. Plan on $400 for a policy.

Offer dog walks at certain times of the day, usually early morning and mid-day. Owners are usually home at night so your work day may be over by 3 p.m.

Leave flyers at veterinary offices, pet shops and groomers.

If you live near an upscale condominium or active-adult retirement area, leave flyers in the community or rental offices.

Pitfalls to Avoid

Time is money. Do not waste it by taking on dogs outside a target zone. You need to be able to get and drop off dogs on foot so your service area should be a radius of a couple miles, depending on your level of fitness.

Do not handle aggressive dogs. Remember you could be sued if a dog under your care attacks a person or another dog. Always meet the dog prior to accepting him as a client and see if he responds to commands and appears socialized to deal with strangers.

Have every human client sign a service agreement giving you the right to walk their dog. Again, use the pet sitters organization for sample forms.

Be careful if you try to walk multiple dogs at one time. Most dog walkers do, but it does increase the probability of dogs fighting one another and of your losing control of them.

Growth Potential & Expansion

Subcontract jobs to other people. There's always a supply of students and housewives who'd like to make some extra money with occasional jobs.

Sell pet products such as raincoats for rainy days and sweaters for cold days. If you have a clever name for your business, you can get your logo printed on them and sell them to your clients.

Competition

Depends on your area.

Keys to Success

You must be dependable and willing to work in bad weather. Fido still needs his morning walk despite the rain, snow, heat and humidity.

Resources

Pet Sitters International
http://www.petsit.com
201 East King Street -King, NC USA 27021-9161
Phone: 336.983.9222

Professional Dog Walkers Association (Canadian group)
http://www.prodogwalker.com/

37 DVDs for Pets

General Concept

You create DVDs for pets. Not their owners, for the pets themselves. These are a great for dogs or cats that have to stay home alone while their owners are working.

Profit Potential

DVDs retail around $19.95 while production costs are around $2. You do the math.

Equipment Needed

You can spend thousands on video equipment. Instead, rent the latest and best equipment. Then have your product professionally duplicated.

That will ensure the DVD or whatever plays on 99.99% of the equipment in America without creating any problems.

Getting Started

Marketing and advertising will be your largest expense. Renting equipment and studio time to do the editing will be in the hundreds. If you aren't a video hobbyist now, take a class at a local community college. You need to learn how to edit your video and that's easier done after you've had a class or two.

Pick a pet—cats or birds are ideal—and create a product for them. Ideally, this will be a type of pet you own so you can test market until you find a winner.

Pitfalls to Avoid

Don't try to duplicate these materials yourself. A paper label you create and put on a DVD may harm the client's DVD player (unlike a CD-ROM where you can usually get away with this). Using a professional company, however, ensures compatibility with almost every player sold.

Growth Potential & Expansion

Approach businesses about using your DVD as a promotion for their business with a "compliments of" cover jacket. Keep adding products in the same line; e.g., more DVDs for cats or birds or whatever pet you specialize in.

Once you have a popular product, get it sold by Wal Mart, Sam's Club/Costco and QVC or Home Shopping Network.

Competition

Not a lot—yet.

Keys to Success

Marketing. Create a compelling website. Send out press releases. Consider advertising in e-zines and newsletters.

Get an Universal Product Code (UPC) (http://www.uc-council.org/) so Amazon and Barnes & Noble websites will carry your product. It is very expensive to get your own UPC.

See if your DVD duplicator will provide one for you. One company that does is Discmakers at http://www.discmakers.com.

DVDs for Pets

Resources

See example of DVDs for cats at:
http://kittyshow.com/bugsdvdinfo.htm
http://www.cattv.com/VideosforCats.htm
http://www.catgift.com/toliettrain.asp

DVDs for dogs:
http://www.speedvd.com/daycaretext.html

38 Electronic Dog Trainer

General Concept

To help the busy, stressed-out or inexperienced dog owner, you can become an electronic dog trainer. Training a dog challenges many owners. Check amazon.com and you'll see how popular dog-training books are.

This is ideal for an experienced dog trainer who has a book or basic service, s/he sells initially. Offer as a follow-on or separate service, an e-mail service so that owners can get advice whenever they need it. Many owners would love to take Fido to weeks of training but don't have the time or travel too much. Instead, make yourself available whenever the owners have the time.

Profit Potential

Charge on a time-basis such as $10 a month or $50 for six-months. People typically need help during the puppy years so rather than long-term clients, you need a constant turnover of new clients. Get payment up front.

If you accept telephone calls as well as e-mails, charge more for the telephone since they restrict your time and make sure the client pays for the call. Do not use an 800-number!

This is not a full-time business but one that can supplement your income if you are an established dog trainer.

Equipment Needed

You need a computer and Internet/e-mail access. It's great to have high-speed Internet access, and it would be a legitimate business expense. In addition, you may want to offer telephone consultations and will need voice mail service.

All the real equipment to be successful is in your head. It will help to develop answers to frequently asked questions such as how long will it take to house train Fido and how do I stop Fido from jumping up on people.

Getting Started

Guarantee to answer e-mail or telephone questions within a defined period, such as within 48-hours although ideally you will answer questions within a few-hours. If you're fluent in any languages besides English, offer your service in that language. Leave flyers in veterinarian offices, doggy day cares, pet stores and upscale neighborhoods. Try to establish relationships with local dog breeders so they will give one of your flyers or brochures to each customer.

Pitfalls to Avoid

Don't charge so little that it's not worth your time to do this and don't try to charge on a per-question basis unless you do it on a website. The bookkeeping would get complicated. Develop a rate for a period of time. Do not offer guarantees; dogs are unpredictable.

Growth Potential & Expansion

This is a nice addition to someone who is already a dog trainer and has a following in a locality. The income probably will be small but so will the investment of your time. A nice advantage is that you now can funnel the people who call asking for free advice to your new e-coaching service.

If you're a recognized expert at least in some locality, you may want to develop a subscription website. You can offer an annual membership or charge per question. This would only require about $300 to set up and could net you a regular, although probably small, income. The right software will take care of the bookkeeping.

Get a PayPal account and possibly a separate merchant credit card service.

If you're not that well known, try to specialize in a certain style of training, such as clicker training, or certain types of dogs, such as hunting/retrievers dogs. People pay for expert guidance and immediate availability.

Competition

None that I know of. Electronic dog training and coaching is new although e coaching is catching on in other fields.

Keys to Success

You make this business go or fail. Demonstrate genuine concern and interest in your clients and their dogs.

Stay up-to-date on the latest training issues and procedures. Your clients will read about, for instance, clicker training in the latest issue of DogWorld, and you'd better be able to answer their questions about it.

Resources

For examples of successful e-coaches in other fields:
http://www.fitnessdesigns.net
http://www.coachtroy.com

39 EMBROIDERY

General Concept

You give your creative talents full run by embroidering pet-related logos, drawings, sayings or other artwork on clothing and other fabric goods. With the advent of computerized embroidery, this has become a business that can be very satisfying as well as lucrative.

Profit Potential

One Minnesota woman made $50,000 doing all the work herself in a four-month period. An Embroidery Monogram Business magazine survey revealed that average annual gross sales were $282,000.

Most companies had a minimum price per piece of approximately $5.

This is a business that isn't often considered but one that can be a good moneymaker if you market aggressively.

Equipment Needed

You need a commercial needle embroidery machine and computer with designs. These machines are not inexpensive. You could easily spend up to $100,000+ on a new one so you might look at leasing one or buying a refurbished one (with a guarantee) to get started.

Toyota products are considered among the top lines of embroidery machines. Another long-time, quality product line is Meistergram. There also are franchises available although you can operate this business successfully by yourself.

101 Home based Businesses for Pet Lovers

Getting Started

Create a few products for yourself or friends. Get a booth or table at nearby pet shows and competitions and take orders for your products. Some embroidery machines are small enough to be portable and you may be able to create products right at the shows.

Also participate in industry trade shows. Booth fees can be expensive so you may want to advertise at local pet shows for someone to share the cost and operation of a booth with you.

This should be a product that complements but does not compete with yours.

Don't limit yourself to dogs and cats. Horses are a major market. Create horse and barn designs, which can be customized with logos and other scripts. You also can personalize horse blankets, hay bags, jackets, caps, shirts, etc. for a stable. Take samples of work to tack and western wear shops.

Pitfalls to Avoid

Don't try to do this with a home, non-commercial machine. You need a commercial embroidery machine to handle the volume necessary to make any money.

Growth Potential & Expansion

Expand to other markets including square dance clubs and riding schools that you reach at western wear and sporting goods stores.

Competition

Depends on your area but is rarely a saturated marketplace.

Embroidery

Keys to Success

Do quality work. That's more important than price. Also meet the deadlines you give your customer no matter how late you have to stay up working.

101 Home based Businesses for Pet Lovers

Resources

Embroidery Monogram Business monthly magazine
(has good website also)
http://www.embmag.com/embroiderymonogram/index.jsp
1115 Northmeadow Parkway
Roswell, GA 30076

Carolina Stitch
(has good discussion board for questions)
http://www.carolinastitch.com/

Meistergram machines are now manufactured by Barudan but they still offer a business opportunity.
http://www.barudan.com

New Business Ventures
Barudan America Inc.
5 Oak Branch Drive, Suite E
Greensboro, NC 27407-2157
Phone: 336.547.6100

Toyota machines have many dealers.
Here's one to start with who also leases machines and offers training programs:
Pantograms Corporate Office
http://www.pantograms.com/
4537 S. Dale Mabry Hwy -Tampa, FL 33611
E-mail: info@pantograms.com

40 Export Consultant

General Concept

You help small and medium size businesses export their pet products to overseas markets. Many companies are overwhelmed by the paperwork involved in trying to export but recognize the potential for increased sales, if they only knew how to reach foreign customers.

You can run your business as an independent agent selling the products overseas, or you may decide to start a freight forwarder business. Freight forwarders arrange shipment of goods to foreign countries and often prepare all the documentation.

One benefit of exporting as opposed to importing is that there are many government resources and agencies available to help you along the way. See also the Importer chapter of this book.

Profit Potential

If you work at it, this business can earn a six-figure income. On the other hand, you may only want to handle one or two clients. Commissions usually range from 5% to 15% of the sales price depending on the cost of the item. With experience, you may become an exclusive export agent for a number of small manufacturers.

Equipment Needed

Research the U.S. Commerce and Treasury Department websites for information on exporting. You must understand (although the freight forwarder can do the documentation) tariffs, duties, shipping, insurance and payment methods specific to international trade. If you are starting with no knowledge, expect to spend several months just learning the basics.

The Federal Maritime Commission http://www.fmc.gov/ licenses ocean freight forwarders while the International Air Transportation Association (a commercial group) http://www.iata.org/index.htm
controls air cargo agents.

Don't act as a freight forwarder for another business until you are licensed. You, however, can act as your own freight forwarder without a license.

Getting Started

Attend trade and pet shows to identify products that could be sold overseas. Again, many companies will not try to export themselves but may be willing to let you do all the work.

Start small. Try exporting to Canada or Mexico and then to the United Kingdom. Once you have some experience, you can venture further into Europe and Asia.

Pitfalls to Avoid

Don't handle products that don't travel well (too fragile or too heavy) or are already widely available overseas or products that do not translate well in other cultures; e.g., dog products are unlikely to be popular in Saudi Arabia.

Learn enough about the cultures of the countries you want to export to so you do not waste time with products that won't appeal to the local markets.

Export Consultant

Growth Potential & Expansion

You can expand your services to products unrelated to pets although you may find pet businesses as much work as you can handle.

Competition

Few export agents specialize in pet products although many markets, such as England, France and Germany, are so pet friendly they are wide open to unusual products.

Keys to Success

Use the best freight forwarder you can find if you don't provide these services yourself.

Identify good distributors in the foreign countries to which you export. Don't try to sell directly to foreign stores or merchants. It's too time consuming. Deal with distributors.

Resources

The National Customs Brokers & Forwarders Association of America, Inc.
http://www.ncbfaa.org/ (offers courses)

1200 18th Street, NW, #901
Washington, DC 20036
Phone: 202.466.0222

International Trade Information Center (U.S. government site)
http://www.ita.doc.gov/
Phone: 800-USA-Trade

The Export Institute of the United States of America (organization offers certifications)
http://www.exportinstitute.com/

6901 W. 84th St., Suite 317
Minneapolis, MN 55438

Also download for free *A Basic Guide to Exporting* from the Office of Export Development, International Trade Administration, U.S. Department of Commerce
http://www.unzco.com/basicguide/

41 Fishless Aquarium

General Concept

You create, sell and set up fishless aquariums in customer's homes or businesses. These really are known as reef aquariums consisting of corals, anemones, and invertebrates.

Real corals and plants can be difficult to maintain and require specialized equipment. such as special metal halide lighting and additional filtration equipment. In developed areas including the U.S., it is usually illegal to harvest coral and almost any other living thing from the ocean. Therefore, it's best if you create and sell reef aquariums using artificial products.

Fortunately, today's artificial or synthetic coral and plants are extremely life like. Sometimes even better than life because they can be molded or shaped into attractive designs with caves and crevices for visual interest.

Artificial coral, plants and rocks will not scratch glass or plastic aquariums, are lightweight, durable and easy to maintain.

This is a great add-on business for a fish-aquarium maintenance or leasing business.

Profit Potential

Even artificial corals and plants are expensive. The cheapest plant typically sells for $5 to $10 each depending on size while each coral is $30 to $70 depending on size. One of the top product lines sells individual pieces from $50 to $200. You might offer three total aquariums at different price points—basic, standard and deluxe. A typical reef aquarium might retail for $1,000 although a Yuppie stockbroker could easily spend $10,000 to get a custom designed one.

Equipment Needed

Aquarium supplies including tank and water filters and artificial coral, plants and rocks. Sample various manufacturers' products to find the ones you like. Then create a sample you can photograph.

Getting Started

See if local pet or fish stores will offer your service. They may be willing to do so for a fee or joint venture with you to sell the products while you actually create and set up the aquariums.

If you have a ready-made reef aquarium, leave flyers with a photo at stores, professional offices and in upscale areas. Try small classified ads in local papers.

Pitfalls to Avoid

Don't add fish. You may be tempted and some customers may ask for it, but this is a fishless system by design. Adding fish requires more of a different ecosystem than the reef aquarium. Because today's coral and plants are more lifelike, they are not as hardy as yesterday's plastic pieces. Do not soak in chlorine bleach the way you might have ten years ago. Follow the manufacturer's recommendations for cleaning.

Growth Potential & Expansion

Offer products that are not easily found so that a customer can be assured he or she has a limited collection that can't be reproduced at Petco. Fishless aquariums are a status symbol.

Fishless Aquarium

Offer a maintenance contract and upgrades (new products) on a semi-annual or annual basis. This is a trendy business, and you need to offer the latest fad.

Competition

Depending on your area, local pet or fish stores may offer this or you may have the field to yourself.

Keys to Success

Read, study, read, study. Even though you deal with artificial plants, you must know enough to simulate a living reef environment and enough to convince potential customers that they should spend thousands of dollars with you.

101 Home based Businesses for Pet Lovers

Resources

Living Color Enterprises (artificial corals, reef for resale)
http://www.livingcolor.com/
306 N. Robertson Boulevard
West Hollywood, CA 90048
Its interactive reef system (called Plug and Play) is about $200 per reef.

Aquaria's SeaGarden artificial plants
http://www.marineandreef.com/shoppro/plants.html
E-mail for information at sales@marineandreef.com

Nature's Image (winner of Petco new product award for fake coral and anemones)
http://www.naturesimageonline.com/
5450 W. 104th Street
Los Angeles, CA 90045

Hagen Exo Terra natural waterfalls and other terrarium items
http://www.hagen.com
(dealerships are available)

42 Freelance Riding Instructor

General Concept

You drive to your client's home or where they board their horses to give riding lessons.

You avoid the need to own school horses, equipment, barn or land. Obviously you need to love horses, know how to ride and be able to teach others how to do it.

Profit Potential

Instructors typically charge $25 to $45 for a one-hour lesson. Charge extra for travel expenses, which may be considerable.

After all, you're probably driving in rural areas with clients miles apart. Charge at least the IRS allowable mileage deduction for the year (e.g., 36-cents a mile).

Equipment Needed

One of the benefits of this business is that you don't need equipment beyond your own riding equipment and clothing, and you can deduct what you do buy as business expenses.

You may need a list of items that you want your students to have, however, and provide brand recommendations.

Getting Started

Join the American Riding Instructors Assn. (ARIA) for $35 (see Resources) and get certified as a riding instructor. Otherwise you will be at a competitive disadvantage. This association also provides networking and marketing assistance.

Many state and agriculture colleges offer courses or certification program in equine instructing techniques and they're not all in the Midwest. For instance, the University of Vermont in Burlington has an excellent program.

Decide if you want to specialize in a certain type of rider or a certain type of riding. For instance, will you handle children, adults, beginners, or advanced students? Can you teach dressage, hunt seat and jumping?

Leave flyers at horse shows, equine veterinary offices, feed stores, western clothing stores and boarding stables, which do not have their own instructors. Your business will grow by word-of-mouth.

Pitfalls to Avoid

Minimize your travel to the degree possible. If you have to drive 50 miles to each appointment, you may only be able to handle three riding lessons a day.

At least 44 states have some form of equine activity liability laws. Have every student sign a liability release (see Resources for a book with templates). Even though you don't own the horses the students are riding, you could be sued if a student has an accident on the basis that you failed to properly supervise the student.

Growth Potential & Expansion

If you have more business than you can handle individually, hire other people to work for you as trainers or serve as an agent for other freelance trainers.

Sell equipment, training materials and clothing to your students.

Freelance Riding Instructor

Competition

This is a competitive business. You need great word-of-mouth to succeed.

Keys to Success

Many people are great with horses and good instructors, but they can't or won't market their services effectively.

Attend horse shows and competitions where your clients are riding. This will help you fine-tune your instruction for clients while enabling you to network and market your services. Clients will be happy to see you take an interest in their efforts.

Resources

American Riding Instructors Association (ARIA)
(a MUST for this business)
http://www.riding-instructor.com
28801 Trenton Court
Bonita Springs, FL 34134-3337
Phone: 239.948.3232

Equine Law & Horse Sense
written by equine law practitioner,
Julie I. Fershtman
(Western International, 1996)
Available at www.amazon.com for $17.95

*Teaching Safe Horsemanship:
A Guide to English & Western Instruction*
Jan Dawson
(Storey Publishing, 1997, 144-pages)
Available at www.amazon.com for $20.97

43 Freelance Writer

General Concept

Love pets, love writing? Combine your loves into a freelance writing career. You can specialize in a certain type of pet or special interest, such as exposing animal rights groups or promoting aromatherapy for pets. You can become known quickly for your specialty and sell articles on your topic to publications beyond the pet market publications.

Profit Potential

So much depends on your energy, marketing and discipline. The major pet publications (Dog Fancy, Cat Fancy) pay $50 to $400 for a published article. Reptiles (a growing market) pays 5 to 10-cents per word while WildBird pays $300 to $500 for a major article.

Don't overlook pet association publications (such as the American Kennel Club Gazette) or veterinary universities that publish consumer publications (Tufts and Cornell). There's also the professional pet market with publications such as *Pet Age* and *Pet Business*.

This is unlikely to be a full-time income but can be a fun part-time business.

Equipment Needed

A computer with word processing software; e-mail and Internet account; telephone with voice mail; a recorder for recording in-person or telephone interviews; and a few reference books.

Freelance Writer

Besides a dictionary and thesaurus, you'll want one or two references about the pet you specialize in. For instance, if you write on dogs, you'll want the American Kennel Club's The Complete Dog Book (get an used copy) with dog breed descriptions, glossary and articles on key dog topics.

Getting Started

Visit your local library and review the latest Writer's Market and other publications that explain how to query editors, format manuscripts and submit articles. Read the magazines you want to query and become familiar with the type of articles they buy. Most publications offer free or low-cost sample issues.

Target a publication and a category, such as grooming or nutrition. Develop an article using an Internet search and a telephone or e-mail interview with a veterinarian or other specialist. If you live near a veterinary college, call their public relations office that will identify veterinary professors for interviews.

Pitfalls to Avoid

This is writing for money, not yourself. Review your target publication so you understand what kind of articles they want - for a general audience or the professional market. You won't be successful until you learn to change your "voice" to match the one the publication wants.

Growth Potential & Expansion

Become an expert by getting numerous articles published. Then approach a book publisher about a book on your specialty. For instance, look at all the "Dummies" and "Idiots" books on animals.

It's amazing how narrowly you can slice topics for books.

101 Home based Businesses for Pet Lovers

Don't overlook the international audience, especially the English-speaking. International magazines are available at larger Barnes & Noble bookstores.

Competition

This is a tough business because there are few publications for each type of pet and other well-known pet professionals (e.g., trainers, groomers) supplement their incomes or increase their name-recognition by writing articles.

You're unlikely to be able to reword and resell articles from a large publication to smaller publications in the same field (a major income source for other freelance writers) because smaller pet publications will assume their readers have already seen your article.

Keys to Success

Perseverance and continual marketing. Once you've sold an article to the pet publication, see if you can revise it for a wider audience publication. For instance, an article in a dog publication on how to provide for Fido in your will could be revised and sold to publications for Baby Boomers or financial publications.

Resources

Dog Writers of America Association, Inc.
http://www.dwaa.org/

Cat Writers' Association, Inc.
http://www.catwriters.org/

American Horse Publications (AHP)
http://www.americanhorsepubs.org/

44 Geese Patrol

General Concept

You use your Border Collie(s) to keep geese off golf courses and other properties. This business was started by a golf course superintendent who discovered his Border Collie chased away the Canadian geese that marred the greens. After a few weeks, the geese, which were not harmed, left for good. The Border Collie's natural instinct is to herd, not attack.

Profit Potential

The founder of this business started it in the mid-1980s and by 2000, grossed $2M in fees with some 25 dogs. A yearlong contract with a large area (city park or corporate campus) typically is $8,000 to $9,000 while weekly fees are $300 to $800, depending on the size of the area and extent of problem. Charge more for a one-week or other short-term lease and offer a discount for a longer-term lease.

It usually takes more than one-week to get the geese to leave for good. If geese have been nesting in an area for a long period, it may take two years of Border Collie patrolling before the geese leave for good.

Equipment Needed

Only Border Collies can do this job. No other breed is right for it. While herding the geese, they use their natural ability to give the geese the "eye," a threatening, wolf-like look that convinces the geese they are in the presence of a predator. The dogs do not attack the birds. The geese just get tired of being "herded" and harassed and leave for greener areas.

This method of geese control has been approved by the USDA Wildlife and Fish Service and the Humane Society. Border Collies are not difficult to find and you don't need a dog show quality pet.

It's best to get a purebred, however, so expect to pay $1000 to $3000. Also try Border Collie Rescue Groups who may have mature dogs available, ideally one who has been trained to herd sheep.

Getting Started

Find a golf course willing to let you do the job for free in exchange for the right to use them as a reference. If your dog isn't already trained for herding, you will need some time to refine his behavior. Once you learn how long it takes and how best to convince geese to move on, you can start charging for your service.

Pitfalls to Avoid

If you've never owned a Border Collie, you may not understand how strong their herding instinct is. They do not make good pets because of this.

If you don't keep your dog busy, he will release his natural behavior by "herding" family members and any other animals within his range as well as chewing everything that he can get in his mouth. A busy Collie is a happy Collie.

The area where you keep your Collie(s) must be zoned properly for multiple dogs. Don't assume you can keep two or three Border Collies in your suburban backyard.

Geese Patrol

Neighbors may complain to authorities.

Growth Potential & Expansion

Market your services beyond golf courses to any business or facility that has large yards and a geese problem. Some companies have hiking or running tracks for employees that become unusable thanks to geese and their dropping.

Other potential clients include universities, city and county buildings, state parks, cemeteries and residential communities.

Competition

There are several businesses operating, mainly on the East Coast.

Keys to Success

Your canine employees make or break this business. It make take as long as a year to train a journeyman-level dog, and you shouldn't put him to work until he's out of puppy hood and about 14 months old. Spend his puppy year socializing him and training him in the normal dog commands.

101 Home based Businesses for Pet Lovers

Resources

Examples of this business:
Geese Police
http://www.geesepoliceinc.com
(the founder - they also sell franchises)

Gooseworks
http://www.thegooseman.com
12040 Crooked Lane Rd
South Lyon, MI 48178
Phone: 810.599.5315

Find a Border Collie rescue group at the American Kennel Club website.
http://www.akc.org/breeds/rescue.cfm

45 GROW WORMS

General Concept

You grow worms, also known as vermiculture. If you don't mind getting your hands dirty and you live in an area where you can keep them, this can be an easy part-time business. Very, very few people make a full-time living from this business, but for some reason (maybe it's a guy thing), it remains a popular one.

One successful website, Wormman Worm Farm, states that it services 1400 bait shops, 780 pet stores and thousands of personal customers.

Profit Potential

Although worms can be used for waste management, animal feed and producing pharmaceuticals, the typical home grower mainly sells them for fish bait or to local pet stores for food. One hundred pounds of redworms usually retails for a maximum of $800.

The other major market is selling compost created by the worms. This organic compost is popular with gardeners, and you may be able to sell it to local garden shops.

The reality remains that worms are usually easier to grow than they are to sell.

Equipment Needed

The Wormman offers a worm breeding kit for $20.95 (see Resources). It comes with two bins, bedding, food, and 250 mealworms (best for fish bait). Instructions also are included.

101 Home based Businesses for Pet Lovers

This will give you an idea whether you like this business and how hard or easy it is for you to do.

The Happy D Ranch offers an elaborate commercial starter kit of information—no worms—for $65.

Fortunately, worms are not expensive to buy and easy to grow. In fact, worm populations usually double in two to four months time. Don't buy too many to start with.

You'll need buckets and boxes to house them while they're growing and worm meal. The size and quantity depends on the size and quantity of the worms you want to grow. Do your homework researching the field before you go out and buy any supplies.

Getting Started

Visit local pet and feed stores and see if they need a local supplier. If you live in a tourist fishing area, see if local sporting goods, convenience stores and gas stations will let you put up a stand there.

Read up on worms and decide what type you want to breed. Most novices start with earthworms, mealworms or redworms.

Try small classified ads in your local newspaper or free newspaper.

Pitfalls to Avoid

Beware of extreme temperatures.

You must protect your worms if you live in cold climates or extremely hot climates although worms can live in those climates. If it's 80 degrees, don't have some shipped to your home if no one's going to be there and the worms are going to sit outside on your doorstep all day in the sun. You'll be sorry.

Grow Worms

Also beware of scams where companies try to get you to buy worms with the promise they will buy back the mature worms. For some reason, the worm business has attracted several buy-back scammers.

Growth Potential & Expansion

Sell products associated with vermiculture/vermicomposting such as bins, harvesters and other vermiculture paraphernalia

Joint venture with a livestock operator. Worms grow in the waste product of the stock animal while the stock animal is pastured on grasses enhanced with worm castings.

Competition

Depends on your area. In some locations, it is a saturated market.

Keys to Success

Finding a market for your worms.

Resources

The Wormman Worm Farm
(also offers an affiliate program)
http://www.wormman.com

The Worm Digest (very good information)
http://www.wormdigest.org
P.O. Box 544
Eugene, OR 97440-0544
Phone: 541.485.0456

Happy D Ranch
http://www.happydranch.com/77.html

46 Horse Boarding

General Concept

You have a large property (or lease one) that enables you to board horses for other owners. This requires a barn for protection from the elements and an area to exercise the horses.

This can be a profitable business for someone who loves horses and already has the right kind of property for it. Competition is declining in this business because of increasing land prices and complaints from homeowners who move near horse facilities.

Profit Potential

Your best chance of success is to live near a suburban area that is being developed rapidly and leaving little land for homeowners to keep horses. Horse ownership has been increasing over the past few years while the number of boarding stables has declined.

This business is unlikely to work if you live in a rural area with many small farms.

Overnight boarding typically runs $20 to $50 a night or $250 to $350 a month, depending on the area of the country. Charge more if you provide full care and offer a lesser amount if you just provide a boarding facility while the owner feeds, exercises and cares for the horse.

Equipment Needed

If you have a large property with barn and acreage, you're set. You can add to it later with refinements like a show ring if you establish sufficient cash flow. If you aren't now living on such a property near a suburban or urban area, this is probably too expensive a business for you to start. Keep reading the other chapters of this book.

You need insurance and written agreements with your boarders. Additional insurance is required if you accept mares in foal. If you let people ride on your property, insist they wear a helmet or sign a waiver.

Getting Started

Research horses and their care so you understand how best to take care of them.

Canvass horse shows, saddle clubs and equine businesses including horse veterinarians and feed stores to see if there is a need in your area for boarding facilities. If there's a market, develop a flyer with your rates and hand them out at the same places.

Develop a sheet or two explaining what horse owners should look for in a good boarding facility, include your contact information on it and leave them at equine businesses. Many store owners and veterinarians like being able to give their customers a free publication with helpful information.

Pitfalls to Avoid

What looks good to a human isn't necessarily good for a horse. We like the look of a barn stall with straw or shavings on the floor but these materials can wick moisture from a horse's hoof and cause them to dry and crack.

The best boarding facilities mimic nature to the degree possible with grass pastures, freedom of movement (within a fenced area) and the company of other horses while providing an indoor barn or stall at night or as the horse desires.

Do, however, make sure you are protecting the horses from predators while they are outdoors.

Growth Potential & Expansion

Team with a good riding instructor(s) who can teach dressage, western and hunter styles of riding. Give the instructors a discount if they board their horses at your stables.

Provide an indoor arena so people can ride at night and all year despite the outside weather. This is expensive to build, but you'll have few competitors.

Associate your business with any nearby upscale housing development. Some builders will like the idea of being able to offer horse-boarding facilities to their homeowners.

Competition

The number of horse boarding facilities has declined because 1) property near urban areas has become so expensive there is more profit in developing it for housing and 2) ban or limitations are placed on the number of horses that can be boarded to satisfy homeowner complaints about smells and noise and environmental concerns such as waste disposal and water usage.

Keys to Success

Develop relationships with an equine veterinarian, pet sitter and farrier who will respond to emergency situations.

Join with other horse boarder or riding facilities to form an association to lobby local government agencies on your behalf.

Resources

EquiSearch—Internet search engine for everything related to horses
http://www.equisearch.com/

Example of local horse boarders association:
Kitsap Barn Owners Association
http://watermarkfarm.net/kboa/

47 Horse Cargo Trailer Service

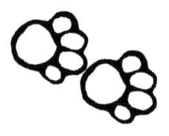

General Concept

You haul horses to shows, fairs and new owners. Not all owners have enough horse trailers to handle this job themselves. If you already love horses and like car trips, this business will seem like a dream job.

Profit Potential

Typical charge is $50 per trip plus mileage (see what the IRS allows).

Equipment Needed

You'll need a trailer (look at leasing) and sufficient insurance both for your vehicle and your liability while the horse(s) is in your control. Trailers are expensive so lease or rent until you develop sufficient business base to purchase one.

Remember horses are expensive, make sure you have a large, umbrella policy.

Getting Started

Network, network, network. Get to know horse owners by attending shows, fairs etc. and passing out your business cards or flyers.

Pitfalls to Avoid

Horses are expensive. The owners need to trust you to do a good job and take care of their animals.

Horse Cargo Trailer Service

Don't accept diseased horses—learn enough about horses to be able to examine them for common illnesses.

Growth Potential & Expansion

Subcontract during peak months such as summertime when many county fairs are ongoing.

Competition

Not many people specialize in this.

Keys to Success

Don't leave horses unattended. Unless you're driving a short distance, you need a second person in the car to watch the horses while you take a break. For overnight trips, one of you should be on duty. Remember, horses can be worth thousands of dollars. You don't want one stolen or hurt on your watch. Do a good job and get referrals.

Resources

Suppliers of horse trailers:
Sundowner of California
http://www.sundownerofca.com/main.html
505 Hilltop Drive
Auburn, CA 95603
Phone: 530.887.9502

Trailers America
http://home.fuse.net/trailersamerica/
2300 E. Kemper Rd.
Cincinnati, OH 45241
Phone: 513.771.1810

48 Importer

General Concept

You import pet products from foreign countries into the United States. You can act as a distributor and sell the products to pet stores and other businesses, or you can sell the products yourself through the mail or Internet.

Although the U.S. government provides a wealth of materials for those who want to export, you will have to do much research yourself to learn how to succeed as an importer. You also may decide to operate a customs brokerage business for yourself and other businesses.

Please read the Export Consultant chapter of this book for related resources.

Profit Potential

This can be a lucrative business if you select products that sell well in the U.S., and you can place them for re-sale. It would be most lucrative—and extraordinarily difficult—to get an exclusive distribution agreement so you are the only distributor in a defined area for a foreign manufacturer.

Equipment Needed

Research the U.S. Commerce and Treasury Department websites for information on importing. You must understand how to use the Harmonized Tariff System and Free Trade Zones.

A recommended approach is to get a customs broker license from the U.S. Customs Service at

Importer

http://www.cbp.gov/xp/cgov/import/
broker_management/brokers.xml

by passing a 4-hour examination given two or three times a year. It costs $200 but if you've learned enough to pass it, you'll be well prepared for this business even if you don't want to be a full-time customs broker.

Don't act as a customs broker for another business until you are licensed. You, however, can act as your own broker without a license.

Get a re-sellers tax certificate from the state in which you operate your business.

Getting Started

Start small.

Import from a country that is accessible to you (nearby and where you speak the language; i.e., Canada or Mexico) and limit yourself to one or two foreign manufacturers or products. When you're comfortable with the process, slowly expand your product line.

A benefit is that trips to the country to find suppliers will be tax deductible as a business expense. Almost every embassy or consulate of a foreign country in the U.S. has trade offices that attempt to mate importers with foreign manufactures. Contact the embassy of your choice; e.g., British Trade Development Office, 845 Third Ave. New York, NY 10022 for information on British products.

Visit local pet businesses to see what they want to handle or create a website and market the exclusivity of your foreign-made product. Many people like the snob appeal of say, English products for their pet.

Importer

Pitfalls to Avoid

Understand tariffs so you don't import a product that will be so expensive there is no market for it. On the other hand, don't try to sell cheap products. Import products with enough snob appeal that you can charge a premium price.

NEVER try to evade tariffs or import duties. The minimum fine if you're caught is usually $5,000.

Growth Potential & Expansion

You might decide to operate a bonded warehouse which requires approval from the U.S. Customs Service and a few hundred dollars for fees, bonds and insurance. This can be a good business, however, if your local area is not adequately serviced as many warehouses or storage facilities do not meet the Customs Service requirements.

Competition

It's time-consuming to accomplish the paperwork necessary to import so you may not have as much competition as you would selling made-in-the-USA products. Specialize in a defined product line or manufacturer to become more easily known in the marketplace.

Keys to Success

Use the best customs house broker you can find if you don't provide these services yourself.

Resources

International Union of Commercial Agents and Brokers (information on contracts used in foreign countries)
http://www.iucab.nl/index.php

Importing into the United States,
A Guide for Commercial Importers (a must read)
Download for free at U.S. Customs Service website:
http://www.customs.ustreas.gov/ImageCache/cgov/content/publications/iius_2epdf/v3/iius.pdf

49 Independent Sales Agent

General Concept

You represent non-competing manufacturers of pet products and sell them to retailers within a defined geographical area. The products you represent are intended for resale to consumers. They are not marketing aids, which are covered by the Advertising Specialties chapter of this book.

Profit Potential

Anyone who can sell face-to-face will never go hungry. If you work at this business, you can break the six-figure income mark. One survey reported that independent sales agents grossed an average of $124,000 by their third year.

Commissions typically range from 3% to 16%.

Equipment Needed

If you haven't sold before, read a couple of books on selling and give it a try in your local area.

Take classes to help build your skills. Many community colleges offer courses in making presentations, image development, selling and marketing.

You will need a reliable vehicle for transportation to sales calls and with sufficient cargo room for your samples.

It's a good idea to have a car with a trunk or privacy panel if you use a van or SUV so your products won't be visible to passer-bys when the vehicle is parked.

101 Home based Businesses for Pet Lovers

Getting Started

If you're using a product that you like for your own pets, contact the manufacturer and see if it has a dealership program. Also review the Resource sections of all the 101 businesses here as many of the suppliers listed are looking for independent sales agents.

All the pet-related business magazines have classified ads where manufacturers seek sales representatives. Also check the Manufacturer Representatives Wanted listings from the American Pet Products Manufacturers Association, Inc. at http://www.appma.org/referral/reps_wanted.asp.

If you join the Manufacturer's Agent association (see Resources), it has a monthly publication with ads.

More and more manufacturers are outsourcing this function. It won't be difficult to find manufacturers to represent. (It will be difficult to find customers.)

Pitfalls to Avoid

Don't make your geographical area so large that you spend all your time in travel or arrange to only travel for two or three days a week so that you start from home and cover your area within a reasonable period of time.

Have sufficient savings for several months of effort. Even if you sell a product right away, the manufacturer may not pay you until it's been paid or the product has shipped.

If you work on commissions, it will be difficult and time-consuming to keep track of what you're owed but that's essential if you want to stay in business.

Also read the chapter in this book on Advertising Specialties.

Independent Sales Agent

Growth Potential & Expansion

As you develop a customer base (it's easier to get manufacturers to let you represent them than it is to find buyers) and develop a reputation, you will be able to add more popular and expensive items. You may be able to arrange for exclusive dealerships for some products.

Competition

Many people try to sell but few become successful at it. If you can do it, you don't have to worry about competition; there will always be room in any market for you.

Keys to Success

Keep your paperwork up to date. You need to do this for tax reasons as well as determining when you're owed for commissions or fees. Get everything—your representation agreements and orders—in writing.

Be careful of handling out-of-state manufacturers unless they have good reputations and a track record. It's difficult to resolve problems five states away.

101 Home based Businesses for Pet Lovers

Resources

Manufacturers' Agents National Association (MANA)
($199 annual membership)
http://www.manaonline.org

P.O. Box 3467
Laguna Hills, CA 92654-3467
Making £70,000 a Year as a Self-Employed Manufacturer's Representative
by Leigh and Sureleigh Silliphant
(Ten Speed Press, 1998, 190 pages)
used copies are available at www.amazon.com for around $15

Selling for Dummies
by Tom Hopkins
(For Dummies, 2nd edition, 2001, 432 pages)
available at www.amazon.com for $15.39

50 Install Doggy Doors

General Concept

You install doggy doors that allow Fido or Fluffy to go outside without human interaction. Target busy upscale and retirement communities.

Profit Potential

Doggy doors can be expensive and vary in price by the size of the dog. Nice doors that can be installed in sliding glass doors can cost up to $200 before any labor. Electronic doors range from $300 to $500.

Equipment Needed

Doggy or cat door kit, hacksaw, screwdriver, mallet, folding rule, file, adjustable wrench, screwdriver, pencil, power drill with spade bit jigsaw, level and nail cutter.

Don't start this business unless you're an experienced handyman around your own home.

Getting Started

This business requires advertising. Start with small classifieds the Pets section of your local newspaper.

"We install pet doors in screens, doors, sliding glass doors and walls. Permanent or semi-permanent doors. Licensed, bonded, insured. Call xxx-xxxx."

Pitfalls to Avoid

Not for all-thumbs types. You're working in people's homes so have a talent for construction before you start. Have liability insurance just in case you damage someone's property.

Growth Potential & Expansion

Lease semi-permanent pet doors for a monthly fee. This is good for renters and people in vacation homes.

Contact manufacturers and buy the door kits wholesale.

Competition

Not many people specialize in this.

Keys to Success

Do a good job! Use door hangars in areas you want to service to promote your business.

Resources

Everything you ever wanted to know about pet doors: http://www.petdoors.com

51 International Pet Travel

General Concept

You offer a newsletter, book or booklet aimed at people who want to take Fido or Fluffy outside of or bring into the United States. The Pet Travel Scheme approved by the European Union countries removed the six-month quarantine requirement. Traveling with pets to and from Europe is now feasible.

Your material should be in electronic and hard copy format. Many people prefer to download immediately while others like a product they can hold in their hands. Satisfy both types of customers.

Profit Potential

Create a newsletter or write a book or booklet on international travel with pets and sell it at your own website and at amazon.com and bn.com (Barnes and Noble).

Use your website to promote the book and bring in direct orders without discounts to book sellers and to sell products or services using affiliate links. Be sure to include links for tours related to or that allow pets.

Equipment Needed

You need a computer with Internet access to do research and software to create your website and materials. See if Microsoft Publisher is sufficient before investing hundreds of dollars in more advanced software products.

Getting Started

Research U.S. Customs, Department of Agriculture, and Centers for Disease Control websites for requirements on traveling here or abroad with pets.

Don't overlook the need to cover all types of transportation (plane, car, boat and train) and offer advice to make the pet the most comfortable. Also include regulations of the major carriers such as foreign aircraft companies and rail service for traveling with pets.

Offer your e-book product to www.booklocker.com.

Pitfalls to Avoid

Triple check to make sure your information is correct.

Be honest with your customers about the problems of routine travel (as opposed to long term moves) with pets. Travel is stressful for pets, and they may pick up diseases not found in their native country and for which they have no immunity. You should include a discussion of the most common of those diseases: babesiosis, erlichiosis, heartworm and leishmaniasis.

Growth Potential & Expansion

Offer updates to your information to keep the material current.

Sell the updates directly from your website. If you are fluent in another language, translate your products and website into the more popular languages such as Spanish, French or Japanese.

Competition

There are many books and several websites on traveling with your pet in the United States, but few address international travel.

International Pet Travel

You might specialize in one area. For instance, a website devoted to traveling to and from Mexico with a pet and offering a Spanish version would have a large market.

Keys to Success

Your website is only to promote your product—newsletter, book, booklet or newspaper. Don't offer so much free information on the website that no one buys your product. You can offer electronic versions of your products on the website and sell them for immediate download using Clickbank (www.clickbank.com) if you don't have a merchant account.

Include a listing of emergency animal hospitals or veterinary associations in your book. This would be a reassurance for travelers and could be made into smaller brochures that you sell for a nominal fee along with an order form inside to order the whole book.

Resources

Website for people wanting to bring animals into the U.S.
http://www.foreignborn.com/visas_imm/entering_us/2bringyourpet.htm

USDA Animal and Plant Health Inspection Service
http://www.aphis.usda.gov/travel/pets.html

For travel to and from the United Kingdom, visit this official website:
http://www.britain-info.org/faq/xq/asp/SID.473/qx/showfaq.htm

See Globetrotting Pets for an example of website that markets a book
http://www.globetrottingpets.com/

52 Lease Ecologically Correct Aquariums

General Concept

No neon-colored plastic plants, no ornaments and no painted or dyed fish. This is an aquarium that mimics the natural environment and is mainly self-sustaining. It may be freshwater or saltwater but will have real rocks and driftwood with live plants. You create these aquariums and lease them to business or professional offices. You also maintain them on a regular basis.

Profit Potential

Leasing and maintenance should be on a monthly basis with fees covering both or identified separately. Develop a rate schedule based on size of the tank, type of fish and the amount and complexity of the maintenance required. Offer three to five pricing packages to clients. Typical fees in my area range from $50 to $100 a month with maintenance another $50 a month.

Equipment Needed

Tank and cabinet stand, neutral-colored gravel, live plants and rock, fish (chosen to client's wishes), aquarium cleaning equipment including high-efficiency protein skimmer and upscale lighting. If you have saltwater aquariums, include invertebrates and corals.

The larger the tank, the easier it is to maintain. Offer a 55-gallon tank as your typical package. Depending on what you already have, you should budget at least $1,000.

Your most expensive purchase will be a van to carry the aquariums and equipment. You can do maintenance alone but will need at least one other person to help carry in and set up aquariums in your client's offices.

The client's location must have adequate circulation and electrical outlets for lighting with a timer and circulation pumps. A top quality filtration system is a must.

Getting Started

Read as much as you can so you understand what an ecologically correct aquarium is and how to care for the living plants and fish that will be in it. Target physicians, dentists, retirement homes, lawyers, banks, restaurants, hospitals, day care centers, private schools and business offices.

Send post cards or brochures announcing your service and for local offices, drop by and leave a business card.

Be prepared to explain the benefits of having such an aquarium in their waiting rooms or lobbies such as keeping children occupied and providing comfort to patients. Carry color photographs of your own or other client's aquarium so potential clients can visualize how it might look in their offices.

Have a stand with your business cards that you leave with every aquarium you provide.

Pitfalls to Avoid

Leave a tips brochure or flyer with your aquarium asking people to not feed the fish or adjust the lights on them—both reasons why fish die. Have a timer for the tank lights and never put more food in the tank than the fish can eat then.

LEASE ECOLOGICALLY CORRECT AQUARIUMS

Growth Potential & Expansion

Offer personalized rock sculptures made from sandstone for clients with their business card, logo or company name.

Offer seminars on creating and maintaining these aquariums.

Competition

Depends on the area of the country; however, there is usually less of a problem with competition as compared to getting clients.

Keys to Success

A balanced natural aquarium is far less time-consuming to maintain and clean and is less likely to promote fish diseases. Maintenance, however, must include grooming plants, removing algae, water spots and fingerprints.

Make sure you match the fish with the water quality of your area. Wherever possible, use maintenance fish such as urchins, hermit crabs, starfish or bottom-oriented fish that help keep the marine aquarium clean.

Resources

Aquarium Fish Magazine (good monthly magazine)
http://www.animalnetwork.com/aquafish/
3 Burroughs
Irvine, CA 92618
Phone: (949) 855-8822
One-year subscription is $15.97

Two good websites:

Robert Fenner's website
http://www.wetwebmedia.com/

The Aquarium
http://www.theaquarium.tv/

53 LIST OR SELL PET BUSINESSES

General Concept

If you already have a real estate license, you can specialize in selling businesses related to pet care or services.

If you aren't licensed or don't want to be, create a website solely for advertising pet businesses for sale. This can be local or national. Create two types of websites: one for relocatable business and one for established storefront businesses in an area.

Profit Potential

Business brokers typically charge 10% (or more) of the selling price of a business.

If you just list businesses for sale on a website (local or national), charge a flat fee to list for x-period of time or a monthly fee.

It's difficult to track and collect if you try to charge commissions for sales and might require you to get into the middle of negotiations or deadlocks between buyer and seller. You also may be violating a state law if you don't have a real estate license—in effect acting as agent without a license—so I don't recommend this approach for payment.

Stick with flat fees for listing/advertising.

Equipment Needed

If you want to sell the businesses yourself, get licensed through your state real estate board and "hang your shingle" with a local real estate or business brokerage office. Warning on the latter—just about every one of them will insist you sign a non-compete agreement meaning you can't offer your services in their geographical area for some period of time.

If you're just going to list or advertise businesses for sale, you'll need a computer with high speed Internet service, an account with an internet service provider and the software to create and administer the website. A digital camera is helpful (less than $300) so you can take photos of local businesses. Then you need typical marketing materials such as business cards.

Getting Started

Once you're licensed or have a website up, contact local businesses in person (preferred approach) or by phone and ask the owner if they'd like to list their business. Note that they can do it anonymously.

Network through business, community and trade groups. Pass your business card out to everyone.

Find buyers through small classified ads in local Sunday newspaper and in commercial publications related to pets (such as Dog World magazine). Some mediums will work better for you than others. Test and monitor the results.

Pitfalls to Avoid

Be sure to note on your website or marketing materials that you are providing an advertising medium only. You cannot guarantee the accuracy of the data in the listing and potential buyers should exercise due diligence before entering into a buy/sell agreement.

List or Sell Pet Businesses

Growth Potential & Expansion

Provide a way for owners to list their businesses without their names and act as the intermediary only for the exchange of contact information.

Add affiliate links on your website for related services or products such as loan companies, consultants, business lawyers, and business appraisers.

Competition

Check with major local pet businesses to see if there's any business broker in your area that specialize in pet businesses. The chances are you will have the field to yourself.

There are some websites that list businesses for sale but not many that specialize in pet businesses.

Keys to Success

Be discreet. Don't talk about the businesses or their owners. Many owners will not want suppliers and competitors to know they're trying to sell their business.

Create a website that is easy to navigate and easy for owners to list their businesses themselves. Get as high a ranking in search engines as possible and if website/business name is clear and specific (e.g. Houston Animal Businesses For Sale), you will fare better in the search engines.

101 Home based Businesses for Pet Lovers

Resources

For information on valuing and buying a relocatable business:
Releasable Businesses Newsletter at
http://www.relocatable.com/

Example of a website offering relocatable businesses for sale:

http://www.bizsale.com/businesses-for-sale/relocatable.ht

International Business Brokers Association
(good materials for sale there)
http://www.ibba.org (membership is $395)
11250 Roger Bacon Drive, Suite 8
Reston, VA 20190

54 Local Portal Website

General Concept

You create and operate a community website and business directory of animal-related businesses in your area. This can work for any size area—make it as large an area (city, county, region, state) as you need to get enough advertisers. You sell listings on the website and charge on a recurring basis such as quarterly or annually.

Your website may contain just a link to the advertiser's own website, or you can offer advertisers a web page that describes their business. Many small businesses want a web presence without the upkeep of their own website.

Profit Potential

Charge enough. You will need to advertise your website offline to get visitors and that requires sufficient cash flow. Typical listing fees range from $199 to $1000 a year.

You can prorate for a recurring billing although you should at least insist on a quarterly listing. That will give the businesses some chance to get noticed by web visitors.

Equipment Needed

You need a computer and reliable Internet Service Provider. Get a domain name that is clear as to what your business is. For instance, if you live in Aquafina, WI; your domain name might be Aquafina Pet Businesses. Don't be cute, be clear.

You'll need software such as Dreamweaver MX to create and maintain the website. You also must establish an advertising budget of at least a thousand dollars to start getting your website name out to your local public.

If you don't have a merchant credit card account, you can use PayPal or third party provider such as `http://www.ibill.com` for recurring billings. Not all third party providers offer recurring payments so select one carefully.

Getting Started

Create your website and add some businesses without charge. No one wants to be the first to advertise so make a 90-day, introductory offer for some businesses (probably those where you know the owner) and get them listed on your website. Then you can show those when you're trying to sign up paying customers.

Send out news releases to all local news media and run small ads in weekly shoppers and local newspapers.

Also see if you can get affordable rates to advertise on local radio talk or news shows (don't advertise on music shows). The best advertising for your website is to run TV ads on local news shows. Check out the rates, often you can get good deals for local-only advertising.

Again, don't bother to advertise on anything other than news and weather shows because that increases the probability that your viewing audience will be locals.

Pitfalls to Avoid

Don't expect to get customers just through the website. You MUST sell this in person by taking a copy of your website pages to local businesses and convincing them to add their business to your Internet directory.

Local Portal Website

Growth Potential & Expansion

This website can easily be expanded to include businesses besides animal-related ones and include other profit centers such as affiliate dating sites or classified advertising.

Competition

Many people will not or cannot sell face-to-face. If you're willing to pound the pavement, you can make a success of this business.

Keys to Success

Advertise and join your local Chamber of Commerce or other community organizations where you can network. Hand out your business cards to every business owner or manager you meet, even those outside the animal-related field.

Give each advertiser a door or window sign with their name and your website URL on it. Ask each advertiser to always include the website URL on all their marketing materials.

101 Home based Businesses for Pet Lovers

Resources

Examples of local websites:

Rochester, MN at http://www.roch.com

Jersey Biz Guide at
http://www.jerseybizguide.com

Be sure to look at all the pages on the jerseybizguide for ideas on related areas where you can get advertising or make money, such as by becoming an affiliate for a related business; e.g., Petco.

Louisville, KY at
http://www.LouisvilleBizGuide.com
Also includes other profit centers on the website.

55 Mail Order Supplies

General Concept

You sell pet supplies, preferably specialized supplies for a certain type of pet, the old fashioned way—through the U.S. Postal Service. Yes, the Internet is huge, but there are still millions of Americans who are not online or who prefer to order through the mail.

Profit Potential

Anything is possible in mail order, from a negative amount as you fail to cover your expenses to a six-figure income. One woman started selling a canvas tote bag with a picture of a horse she designed herself. Ten years later, she has a catalog filled with horse-themed merchandise and sales in the seven figures.

Equipment Needed

Get a reseller's permit from your state and information on how to collect sales tax. Spend your time writing a great sales letter and getting great photographs of your product.

Getting Started

The woman with the horse-themed merchandise started by placing the smallest display ad in *Horse Illustrated* magazine. She got 150 requests for information about her tote and made slightly more than $1,200 in sales. She continued to repeat the process.

101 Home based Businesses for Pet Lovers

The two-step marketing technique is the way to go. People usually won't order anything over $10 just based on an ad from a company they don't know. Use your print ad to have people contact you via mail or phone to get a full sales pitch.

Offer the information on your product free but make the potential customer request your product information via mail or phone. Never use an 800-number. You do not want to attract the people who just want something free. Make them pre-qualify themselves by spending the time and their money to write or call for information.

Pitfalls to Avoid

Make sure there's a market for your product. Visit a nearby library that gets Standard Rate and Data Service (SRDS) reference book (it's expensive). In it you'll find what pet-related products consumers have purchased in the past 30, 60 and 90 days and what they paid for them. You want to target a market that is willing to pay for a product you can provide.

Charge enough for your products. Eight times basic cost is not unheard of. Don't sell products that are so fragile or so heavy they are difficult to pack and expensive to ship.

Growth Potential & Expansion

If you create your own product, you can try to get included in other people's catalogs. Get a copy of the Catalog of Catalogs and contact related catalogs. This may be preferable to creating a catalog of your own which can be very expensive.

Also try to get your product on Home Shopping Network or QVC. This is easier than it sounds because they are always looking for new, high-quality products. Check their websites for information on how to submit your product for their review.

Mail Order Supplies

Competition

Many, many competitors. You won't survive trying to compete against PetsMart or Petco. You must target a niche and provide products that are too specialized and too expensive to sell at the pet superstores. Thousands sell toys for dogs and cats but few sell toys for gerbils or ferrets.

Keys to Success

Be sure to take advantage of the many free services the U.S. Postal Service offers at
`http://www.usps.com`.
This includes FREE training, publications and mailing supplies if you ship via Express or Priority mail. Also use the Postal Service for international shipments.

Test, test, test. Never stop tweaking and testing your advertising, letters and products.

101 HOME BASED BUSINESSES FOR PET LOVERS

Resources

How to Start a Home Based Mail Order Business
by Georganne Fiumara
(Globe Pequot Press, 1996, 226-pages)
$12.57 at www.amazon.com

How to Start & Operate a Mail Order Business
by Julian L. Simon (the bible of mail order)
(McGraw-Hill, 1993, 538-pages).
Out of print but used copies are available at amazon.com and possibly at your local library.

Direct Marketing Association (premier trade association but very expensive, visit the website for information on latest laws and possible purchase of reference materials)
http://www.the-dma.org

National Mail Order Association
(for the small to medium size businesses)
http://www.nmoa.org
2807 Polk St. NE
Minneapolis, MN 55418
Phone: 612.788.1673

56 Make Book Marks

General Concept

You create laminated bookmarks with Fido's picture and biography on it or bookmarks with tips for pet owners (example—"7 Problems that Require Immediate Vet Care") as marketing products for other pet businesses.

Profit Potential

Bookmarks can sell for as much as $5 apiece.

The Internet business (see Resources) referenced here sells bookmarks for $1.30 apiece. Charge more if you're creating individualized bookmarks for one pet.

Once you have the equipment and you've figured out how to set up your software, this is an easy business to run.

Equipment Needed

You need a computer with desktop publishing software, photo editing software (such as Microsoft Picture It), clip art or your own photographs. You'll also need a laminating machine (around $200).

You'll need a color printer such as an inkjet with the newer, non-smear color inks.

Use high-quality gloss paper for your bookmarks and then laminate them. An alternative is to use Photo Silk Fabric and apply a photo finishing spray to set the ink rather than laminate it.

101 Home based Businesses for Pet Lovers

Getting Started

Develop a design for the bookmark. A standard size is 2 x 7 inches.

Develop a bookmark for each of the American Kennel Club's or the Cat Fanciers' Association 10 most popular breeds. Include a clip art photo or drawing and information on the breed or tips for caring for the breed.

Sell the bookmarks on eBay as well as at local craft fairs and flea markets. See what type of designs sell the best. Sell individual bookmarks or in packages of five or ten.

Pitfalls to Avoid

Don't violate any copyright laws. You can't use celebrity photos or copyrighted photos or cartoons without the owner's permission (which usually requires royalty fees). Make sure you use clip art that allows you royalty-free use or take your own photographs. Another good source is U.S. government photographs that can be freely reproduced.

Growth Potential & Expansion

Your goal should be to wholesale bookmarks to retail businesses and pet professionals by customizing them. You want to be able to make one design, say for a popular groomer, and then have 100+ reproduced.

Take some samples around to local businesses. Once you have some winning designs, create a website to sell them.

Kids love bookmarks with animals. Use clip art with cartoon animals and add some rhyme or pun. Laminate them and sell at craft fairs and flea markets. For even more interest, you can

Make Book Marks

punch a hole at the of the bookmark and tie a piece of yarn through it to create a tassel.

Competition

There are other bookmark producers but none that I found who specialize in the pet trade.

Keys to Success

Finding enough places to market this product and getting some wholesale accounts.

Market constantly.

Resources

For an example of someone doing this-
Creative Bookmarks
http://www.creativebookmarks.com
1092 Heffner Lane
Reading, PA 19605
Phone: 610.916.9122

Handmade for Profit
by Barbara Brabec
(M. Evans and Company, Inc., 372-pages, 2002)
Available at www.amazon.com for $14.95

National Craft Association
http://www.CraftAssoc.com
E. Ridge Rd. #120
Rochester, NY 14622
Phone: 800.715.9594

Paper for bookmarks—Burlington Paper Products
http://www.burlingtonpaper.com/printingtips/item482.html (fabric)
http://www.burlingtonpaper.com/printingtips/item468.html (glossy paper)

57 Make Electronic Photo Albums

General Concept

You get photos from customers of their pets and convert them into electronic "photo albums" that can be emailed, printed or posted to the Internet. The right software enables you to merge photos, audio, video, and text to build unique, multimedia programs. This goes well with the current popularity of scrap booking.

You also can create hardbound versions of the albums. For the electronic version, each photo will appear on a computer or TV screen for approximately six seconds while music plays in the background. Plan on a maximum of 25 photos per song.

Profit Potential

One company, specializing in weddings, offers a photo album of 120 photographs for $99, which includes music and text. Another charges $1.35 per photo plus additional fees for music, title and end screens and $6 per video clip. You can offer add-ons such as screen savers and desktop wallpaper for another $20 or paper bound volumes for another $50.

Equipment Needed

You need a computer with Internet connection. Have plenty of memory for the graphics programs you'll need. Include hardware and software to create CD and DVDs.

Digital camera if you want to take photographs of local pets ($300 max) plus clip art ($50).

101 Home based Businesses for Pet Lovers

Copyright-free music. A good source is `http://www.elitevideo.com`.

Software to create photo albums and screen savers ($100 max) plus photo software to reverse, tone and size the image.

You can go for a high-end product like Adobe Photoshop but a cheaper product such as Microsoft Picture It will do just fine.

Getting Started

Create a photo album for yourself or a member of your family. You need a great looking one to serve as an example of your work.

Create a website and put your sample album on it. Get your site ranked as high as possible in search engines. Submit to each search engine individually; do not rely on software bulk submissions.

Distribute flyers to local pet stores, veterinarian offices, animal breeders, feed stores, animal shows and try small classified ads in your Sunday newspaper. It may be easier to target one or two types of pets to start with and expand later. For instance, target horses and equine businesses and professionals. Later expand to cats or cattle.

Pitfalls to Avoid

Make sure any photos, text, video or music you use in the albums are copyright free or given to you by the copyright holder. Have each customer sign a form that states they own the copyright to or have licensed the material they are giving you to use. Visit `http://www.nolo.com` to buy some forms.

MAKE ELECTRONIC PHOTO ALBUMS

Growth Potential & Expansion

Add enhanced capability such as Flash and 3-D effects.

Also offer the paper version in a hardcover book, permanently bound with linen or leather covers surrounding heavy, glossy pages that contain photos and text. You design these books on a computer, order them over the Internet, and receive them in a few days. Each 10-page book costs as little as $29.95 (leather is $10 more), and each additional page costs about $3.

You'll need Adobe Photoshop Album for PCs ($50) and Apple's iPhoto software ($50) for Macs. Both companies (Adobe and Apple) let you order the hardbound copies at their websites.

Expand beyond the pet market and sell local businesses or professionals on the idea of creating advertisements or marketing tools with these photo albums. Target businesses related to pets to get started.

Competition

Many sites are producing these but few target pet owners exclusively.

Keys to Success

Your creativity and marketing make you succeed or fail.

Resources

Photo Album Pro Digital Album software ($50)
buy from http://www.provantage.com/

Adobe Photoshop Album
http://www.adobe.com

Apple for iPhoto2
http://www.apple.com

58 Make Keepsake Pillows

General Concept

You combine your interest in photography and sewing into developing keepsake pillows. A photograph of Fido or Fluffy scanned onto photo transfer paper is ironed onto a pillow. Surround with lace, buttons and bows for a nostalgic look.

Profit Potential

This is a luxury item designed for older, mainly female, pet owners. Try selling one you finished on eBay to see what the market might be but have a reserve of at least $30. Auction the pillows under two or three different categories to see which fetches the best price but definitely place it in Collectibles.

Equipment Needed

You need a computer with an inkjet printer. You need to get a photograph into the computer. You can do that with a scanner or a digital camera. I have had better luck taking a photograph of a photograph with my digital camera rather than scanning, but try both approaches. Rent a digital camera to try it and go to Kinkos to have them scan a photo. See which one you like better.

You need photo software to reverse, tone and size the image. I like to create a sepia tone to the photograph. You can go for a high-end product like Adobe Photoshop but a cheaper product such as Microsoft Picture It will do just fine.

Supplies include iron, pillow stuffing, photo transfer paper (from an arts & craft or quilting store), thread, lace, buttons (or whatever you decide to use for decoration), sewing machine, white or light colored cotton fabric and binding. The best fabric to use is off-white, cotton blend.

Getting Started

Develop a design for the pillow. You can let the client provide a pillow or buy one. Decide how you want the photo to be displayed and what kind of decorative effects you will use. You can even sew Fido's old favorite toy (once you clean and sterilize it) to the pillow.

Have a client provide you with a clear photograph of their pet. Scan it or use a digital camera to get the photograph into your camera. Convert the photo to black and white and reverse the image.

Print on a plain piece of paper to test how it looks. Once you're satisfied, using the inkjet printer, print your photograph on photo transfer paper. Trim as needed.

Iron the image onto your fabric, image side down in the desired position. Do NOT use steam, just a hot iron. Iron all the edges and the entire surface. Let the transfer cool.

Carefully peel transfer backing off, starting at one corner. Use the smoothest motion possible.

Then let your creative juices flow and decorate the fabric with all the trims and objects you want. Sew binding to the front of the pillow top.

Put the facing sides together, pin and sew front and back together. Leave a space at the bottom to insert the pillow stuffing. Turn pillowcase inside out and inset the form.

Finish by closing the pillow with a few hand stitches.

Make Keepsake Pillows

This may sound complicated but try it and see how easy, but time consuming, it is to do.

Pitfalls to Avoid

This is time consuming especially the first few times you make one. You'll spend all day on the first one. Don't put too low a price tag on this. This is not a mass produced item, and people are paying for a unique gift item. Get at least 50% of your charge upfront before you start the project for someone.

You don't want to spend so much time and get stiffed by a client. You might even insist on 100% payment before starting the project.

Growth Potential & Expansion

Hire other people to do the work and concentrate on marketing the product.

Teach other crafters/pet owners how to do this.

Competition

None that I found on the Internet.

Keys to Success

Finding enough places to market this product. You may soon tire of making these and want to limit your production to a few a month or even less.

Try to leave samples at pet cemeteries and vet offices. This is an idea keepsake for a pet owner who has a deceased pet.

Resources

National Craft Association
http://www.CraftAssoc.com
E. Ridge Rd. #120
Rochester, NY 14622
Phone: 800.715.9594

59 Mobile Pet Grooming

General Concept

With a specially equipped van, you groom pets at their homes. To groom, you need training from a school or via PETsMART or Petco. If you're untrained, offer no more than washing and minor grooming (e.g., nail cutting) services.

Profit Potential

Check with grooming companies in your area and then add a surcharge because you go to the pet's home. This is less stressful for the pet and a boon for busy or homebound pet owners.

Typical charges are $40 to $50 to groom a dog plus 15% service charge to come to the home. Service six dogs a day and you can make more than $5,000 a month working just five days a week.

Equipment Needed

Dependable van or motor home outfitted as a grooming salon. That includes tub, heating system for van and tub, air conditioning, water tanks and electric service plus normal grooming tools.

If you're in a rural area, you can use a larger van. If you're in an urban area, make sure your vehicle can fit in narrow city streets and home garage driveways. Make sure all equipment meets local and state codes. Have your company name, phone and website (if you have one) painted on your van so it's a rolling billboard. Project Startup Costs To outfit an existing van expect to pay close to $10,000. Buying and outfitting a new one can cost $34,000 to $60,000 with 10% down expected.

If buying new, check with Ford and Chrysler as both offer good financing terms, better than most banks, for vehicle and conversion packages.

Liability and vehicle insurance will run $100 to $200 month depending on your area with vehicle maintenance and gasoline another $100 to $200 a month.

Getting Started

See if your city or state has a requirement or special licensing for those who call themselves a "groomer."

Use door hangers in upscale neighborhoods, active retirement areas (e.g., Del Webb Sun Cities) and condominium/apartment offices.

Be sure all marketing materials state which geographical areas you service (by zip code or name) and include a price schedule. This pre-screens clients and doesn't annoy those who don't want to be bothered having to call to get prices.

Pitfalls to Avoid

Don't service too large a geographic area. You'll waste time traveling and spend too much in vehicle expenses.

Growth Potential & Expansion

Sell grooming supplies and pet food.

Competition

Depends on your area. This is a hot occupation.

Mobile Pet Grooming

Keys to Success

Dependable, good service. It's a plus if you don't need to plug into the homeowner's electric circuits or to dump dirty water on their driveway.

If your customer base is in the city or suburbs, don't select a vehicle that will be difficult to park or maneuver down city streets and in suburban driveways.

Resources

Professional Mobile Groomers International
http://www.yourpmgi.org
784 Morris Turnpike, No. 195
Short Hills, NJ 07078
Phone: 866.BE MOBILE

For insurance policy designed for mobile groomers
Gibson-Governor Agency, Inc.
http://www.gibsongovernor.com
P.O. Box 119
972 Youngstown Kingsville Rd
Vienna, OH 44473
Phone: 330.539.6332

Good resource website: http://www.petgroomer.com/

60 ONLINE DATING SERVICE

General Concept

If you're single or know someone who is, you probably already are familiar with online dating services. This is a great opportunity for you to establish a website devoted to animal lovers especially one targeted to one geographical area.

It's great to find a potential mate who loves iguanas as much as you do but if you live in New Mexico and s/he lives in Maine, you may not have much of a future. How much better to go to a website that handles only pet owners in New Mexico.

You also might target animal lovers who speak Spanish or have some other affinity in addition to having pets.

Profit Potential

Most Internet dating sites charge between $12.95 and $49.95 a month for premium memberships. The annual rate works out to $150 to $600, but even the smallest niche dating sites often have as many as 500 premium members. Do the math.

Equipment Needed

Your biggest expenses will be specialized software to run the dating site and a one-time fee for a technical type to install it. Budget around $500.

Your recurring costs will be credit card fees (you must offer recurring billing via credit cards), site hosting costs and marketing.

Online Dating Service

Getting Started

Join one of the large Internet dating sites such as www.match.com and see how it operates. Make a note of the features you like and ensure you have those in your own site.

Decide on your target market. You can be national—dating site for people who love horses—or regional—dating site for Texas residents who love horses or some combination thereof.

Select a name and get a hosting service. Do NOT be too cute with the name. It should be clear as to what your site is about. For example, Texas Horse Lovers.com.

Get your own credit card merchant account. Both Costco and Sam's Club offer reasonable rates and look at your local bank and Wells Fargo as well.

Send news releases and buy small classified ads in publications that are read by your target market. Leave flyers at animal shows, stores and professions that relate to your site.

Pitfalls to Avoid

If you choose the right niche market, you can grow and grow. If you pick a market that's too broad, you're likely to lose out to the larger general interest sites such as www.match.com.

Whatever market you select, do NOT price memberships too low. You want stable people who are serious enough about looking for someone to pay a significant monthly fee.

Growth Potential & Expansion

Create affiliate sales opportunities. Many animal-themed websites that appeal to your market would be willing to have your link if you offer a small percentage of each membership signup fee. Look at match.com and other large affiliates to see what the going rate is.

Competition

There are many, many dating websites but most are general or national markets. Don't try to compete with an existing website, find a target market that isn't served yet.

Keys to Success

Your Internet website should offer a discussion forum, chat area, search capability and member profile creation with photos and nickname. Use photos of real people (from clip art services such as http://www.comstock.com/web/default.asp) rather than cartoons or stick figures.

Warn members not to give out personal information too quickly and provide a means that clients can contact one another anonymously until they are ready for personal contact.

Online Dating Service

Resources

Look at successful sites:
The two below probably have the largest memberships
http://www.match.com
http://www.matchmaker.com

Examples of niche sites:
http://www.cmle.com (classical musical lovers)
http://www.singlec.com (single Christians)

Examples of software to operate site:
MATCHMASTERS
http://www.planetcgi.com/scripts/matchmasters.html
MojoPersonals 3
http://www.mojoscripts.com/products/
mojopersonals-mysql/dating_software.shtml

61 Operate a Pet Retirement Home

General Concept

You provide the loving care aged pets can no longer get from their owners. Pets may be placed with you because the owners have died or are too ill themselves to care for the pets. The sad truth is many people outlive their pets and have made no provision for their after care.

If you live in a rural area with sufficient land, this is a business that is very satisfying to operate. It's best if you incorporate as a non-profit corporation and can solicit grants and donations to help operate. This also provides liability protection as you care for some seriously ill pets in precarious conditions.

Profit Potential

The profit in this business is in the satisfaction you get from caring for pets that truly need you. You may cover your expenses and draw a salary, but you won't get rich.

Your fees should be based on the age, health and expected lifespan of the pet as well as how many pets you care for in your home. If you have too many pets at one time, you may need to hire people to help you, which will reduce your income. If you have too few pets at one time, your expenses per pet (mortgage, utilities, insurance, vet bills, etc) may be so high per pet that few owners can afford you. You may charge a one-time free for elderly owners who want to provide for their pets or a monthly fee for people who may be temporarily unable to care for their pets. One retirement home for cats charges $170

Operate a Pet Retirement Home

a month or $1,500 annual fee for cats with no health problems. Another charges $10,000 as a lifetime fee.

Equipment Needed

You should own a home with a large yard or acreage if you're going to accept horses. You must be zoned to house multiple animals.

Your yard must be fenced and secure, and the more remote you are from neighbors and traffic, the better.

The major "equipment" you need are your compassionate care coupled with your ability to deal with the deaths of pets you've grown to love.

Getting Started

It's absolutely essential to have legal help in forming your non-profit corporation and preparing contracts that owners sign to authorize and fund the long-term care of their pets.

Some 16 states, from New York to Alaska, now allow pet owners to provide trust funds to take care of their pets after the owner's death. Your lawyer can determine if you can act as a trustee or if it would be better to have a contract for the pet's lifetime care.

Pitfalls to Avoid

You must charge enough. Aged, ill pets require monthly vet care as well as special diets and regular dental care.

You must provide a quiet, comfortable home. Do not have so many pets (even if you find it difficult to turn one away) that you unintentionally create a stressful environment.

101 Home based Businesses for Pet Lovers

Growth Potential & Expansion

If this does not sound too gruesome, you may establish a pet cemetery or memorial park.

Competition

There are very few retirement centers for pets. Those that exist are primarily part of large non-profits such as ASPCAs or state veterinary colleges. You might even be able to contract with one of those to operate the retirement home for them and let the school or organization handle the financial transactions with the pet owners.

Keys to Success

If you operate as a non-profit, it would be helpful to gain support from a national or local celebrity. For instance, the horse retirement home in Resources cares for a horse once owned by former Miami Dolphins quarterback Dan Marino. Mr. Marino not only has been a generous donor but has also participated in fund-raising charitable events.

Operate a Pet Retirement Home

Resources

Examples of pet retirement homes:
For cats and dogs
http://www.bideawee.org/retirement.asp
Bide-A-Wee, Manhattan
410 East 38th Street
New York, NY 10016
Phone: 212.532.4455

For horses
http://www.millcreekfarm.org
Retirement Home for Horses, Inc.
P.O. Box 2100 - Alachua, FL 32616-2100
Phone: 386.462.1001

62 Organic Catnip Products

General Concept

Follow the trend for holistic pet care by offering one or more products (not food) made from organically grown catnip.

Profit Potential

How creative are you? Develop a product line including expensive gift baskets. Later on, sell distributorships to other home-based entrepreneurs.

Equipment Needed

Organic catnip you buy or grow yourself. Pick a distinctive logo for your products and design some toy with the catnip or sell plain catnip in a clever container such as old-time tobacco drawstring pouch with a cartoon cat chewing tobacco on the front.

Getting Started

Contact your state agriculture department to understand what your state requires to advertise a product as "organic." If you live near a state college with an Extension Service, pay them a visit and get loads of inexpensive brochures and advice.

Visit a Small Business Administration office in your area and make an appointment to discuss your projected business with a SCORE volunteer. This is a FREE service to you.

Pitfalls to Avoid

Too many products at once and never updating or adding to your line. Start slowly and add products to your line gradually.

Organic Catnip Products

You need to add a product or new design at least once a year to remain competitive.

Growth Potential & Expansion

Get independent salespeople to market your products.

Competition

Lots. Make sure you test your products on as many cats as possible. Owners will buy what their cats like.

Keys to Success

Clever packaging designs and a marketing theme that appeals to owners.

Resources

American Pet Products Manufacturers Association, Inc.
http://www.appma.org/
for information on laws and marketing
255 Glenville Road
Greenwich, CT 06831
Phone: 203.532.0000

Suppliers:
http://www.kookykat.com/

Grow your own:
http://www.gardenersnet.com/herbs/catnip.htm
http://homeharvestseeds.com/ferrymorseherbscl.htm

Sample website:
http://www.catnipqueen.com/

63 Paw Casts

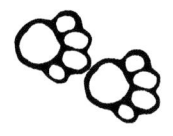

General Concept

You've heard of people who have casts of their baby's hands and feet? You offer a similar service and product for pet owners who think of their pets as their children. This, however, is a business that needs to be done locally.

Profit Potential

Companies that do this for babies usually charge about $80 for a one hand mounted cast and $145 for two hand mounted cast.

You need to cost your supplies. If you aren't going to do the framing yourself, you need to make arrangements with a framing business to give you a substantial discount in return for a certain volume of business. Learn how to do it all yourself to make the most money.

If you're going to mail the finished product, you must add sufficient charges for shipping, packaging materials and insurance.

Equipment Needed

You use a Play Doh like substance to get impressions of Fido or Fluffy's paws, make a plaster case from it and spray paint it gold. Mount the cast in a frame if small enough or in a Plexiglas frame if larger. Visit local craft shops like Michael's to get everything you need.

Getting Started

Set up a table at a local flea market and see if there's a demand for this. Have customer's pay in advance before you make an impression of their pet's paws and then send them the finished product.

Another great market are pet shows where proud owners of prize winners may be happy to memorialize Fido's paws with his prize ribbons.

Once you've made a couple of these, take some photos and incorporate them in flyers that you leave in pet-related businesses including groomers and breeders.

Pitfalls to Avoid

Get payment up front. Once you've sent the finished product to someone, it will be difficult to collect any unpaid charges, but you need cash flow to be able to buy supplies.

Require customers to muzzle large dogs or those that seem agitated or aggressive. Good luck with cats. It's best to wrap them in a towel or blanket and have the owner hold them while you try to get a paw impression.

Also ask the customer if the pet has any known allergies. You don't want to use a product on a pet that might cause a bad reaction. It's a good idea to put this statement with the owner's response on the bill of sale so you can verify that the customer was asked about this.

Growth Potential & Expansion

You can offer a range of frames from basic to very expensive. You also can do real gold plating at a substantial additional charge.

You also can offer to make plaster casts of children's feet and hands as well as other objects. Many women like to have a cast made of their pregnant belly.

Competition

You should have the market to yourself.

Keys to Success

Getting your business known to people is the trick. As this is a luxury item, it is a good one to donate to charitable auctions such as those for private schools or children's hospitals. This helps get your product known to wealthy customers.

Resources

For an example of a similar business:
Twinkle Toes at http://www.twinkletoes.com.au
Basic product is around $100

To learn gold-plating techniques:
Gold Effects offers business opportunity for $1,500
http://www.goldeffects.com
13100 56th Ct, Ste.
701—Clearwater, FL 33760

64 PET ASTROLOGER

General Concept

You provide pet owners who treat their pets like children with an opportunity to learn more about their pets than they could otherwise. If you already understand astrology or have an interest in it, this could be a pleasant way to supplement your income.

Profit Potential

One pet astrologer charges $75 for a personal, one-hour telephone reading. Another Internet site offers printed reports for $10. A third website offers individual, monthly forecasts for your pet at $9.95. Another only handles feline horoscopes.

In other words, whatever the market will bear depending on your skills and ability to distinguish your service from all the rest.

Equipment Needed

If you already have an interest and knowledge in astrology, all you need to get started, besides the basic business licenses, is a website and some marketing materials.

If you're interested in astrology but lack training, start with *Astrology for Dummies* and then expand your knowledge with more advanced works. You also may be able to network with other astrologists and New Age types in your community through stores or organizations that cater to this market. Depending on your skill and needs, you may want software to help you develop horoscopes. (That also requires a computer with

101 Home based Businesses for Pet Lovers

Internet access.) There are two types of software programs: 1) calculate but does not interpret; and 2) produces interpretation reports. Check out any program before you decide to buy. Price will vary depending on features.

Getting Started

Hang out your shingle and get started. Try doing friends and family pets first. Then work a crafts fair or flea market and try your service with strange pets.

Pitfalls to Avoid

Do not run afoul of any laws. Check with a local attorney before you start this business so you don't overlook some local ordinance that could prohibit this business.

Given the horrible publicity and reputation of 1-900 lines, do not offer a $x-a minute call in service. There are pet astrology services that do this, but it's probably just a matter of time (no pun intended) before a federal or state agency cracks down on them.

Growth Potential & Expansion

Develop an Internet-based following and try to syndicate a column on pet astrology for various pet publications.

Develop an easy-to-use software program targeted for pets that you can sell to other astrologers.

Sell related materials (books, crystals, etc) on your website or take them with you when you work a fair or outdoor market.

Competition

Much competition on the Internet. If you do only local readings at fairs and shows, you may not have much competition.

PET ASTROLOGER

Keys to Success

Always advertise and note in your marketing materials: For Entertainment Purposes Only. We are unable to offer guarantees about your pet. Put this in easily readable, bold type. You do not want to run afoul of state or local laws related to fortune telling, which usually includes astrology. You may firmly believe in astrology but most police departments and prosecutors do not.

Resources

Astrology for Cats (Great Quotations, 1998, 168-pages)
Astrology for Dogs (Great Quotations, 1999)
both books are by Simone Reyes and out-of-print although both can usually be ordered from $6 from www.amazon.com

Cosmic Canines: The Complete Astrology Guide for You and Your Dog
(Native Agents Series) by Marilyn Macgruder Barnewall
Attempts to identify the best people-pet zodiac sign combinations. Fun to read.
(Ballantine Books, 1998, 368-pages)
Used from $2 at www.amazon.com
Check out software at
http://www.astrology-software.net/ and
http://www.ukhoroscopesguide.co.uk/netguide/PPF/UK_Horoscopes_Guide/Astrology_Software/GCID/1641/Guide.asp

65 Pet Bakery

General Concept

If your baking makes your dog or cat sit up and beg, you may be suited to a full-time bakery business. There's a market for premium treats for Fido and Fluffy, but it's a highly regulated business.

Profit Potential

The sky's the limit. Retail premium treats (in my area) range from $2 to $5 a piece. Although easy to enter, staying legal is complex. Expect legitimate competitors to turn you in if you become successful without proper labeling and lawful marketing.

Equipment Needed

Does your state require you to use a commercial kitchen or can you do this at home? Believe it or not, even treats are regulated by the Food and Drug Administration if you sell interstate and by state agencies if not. For instance, both California and Minnesota have strict rules on labels for dog and cat treats. Research this area thoroughly.

Liability insurance could be thousands of dollars a year depending on where you live. Shop around for rates.

You must protect your assets by having sufficient insurance and/or incorporating.

Pet Bakery

Getting Started

Interested in a franchise? Visit Three Dog Bakery website. (See Resources)

Otherwise, start with your local Small Business Administration office and find out what laws and regulations affect you.

This is a difficult business to enter because it is so regulated. There are federal laws if you plan to sell through the mail as well as state and local ones. Most communities require you to use a commercial kitchen—not your home kitchen—even to make pet treats if you're going to sell them commercially. Check out the laws in your area.

Try selling your products at dog or cat shows, festivals, flea markets and fairs to see what sells and what pets like. When you get a line of a few products, try to wholesale to pet stores and tourist stores.

Pitfalls to Avoid

Don't try to sell the same thing everyone else is.

Be creative and unique. Specialize in something like birthday "cakes" for dogs or cats. Create doggie or kitty fortune cookies.

Growth Potential & Expansion

Sell organic products. Develop a do-it-yourself kit with all the dry ingredients you need to make a treat plus recipe. Wholesale to non-chain pet stores, groomers, pet sitters and other pet professionals by adding their names on the labels.

Competition

Much competition so find a niche and market constantly. Participate in fundraisers and events at the local animal shelters, dog/cat shows and animal hospitals.

Keys to Success

Cleverness in name and packaging and continuous marketing.

Resources

Sample websites:
http://www.bowmeowbakery.com
http://www.threedogbakery.com

Government:
http://www.fda.gov/cvm/index/animalfeed/petfoods.htm

Industry:
http://www.petfoodinstitute.org
http://www.aafco.org/main.html
(Association of Animal Feed Control Officials, Inc.)

66 Pet Carpentry

General Concept

If you're already a handyman or woman and enjoy carpentry, specialize in custom products for pet owners. These make a home more enjoyable and adaptable to the owner's pets.

For example, dog breeders need whelping boxes and movable outdoor runs. Owners of both dogs and cats may like a two-story feeder: the lower half for dogs and the upper one for cats. Other pet owners may appreciate a special bed, ramp for aging pets or custom awnings to shade the pet outdoors. Trophy cases and foldable grooming benches are other popular products.

Profit Potential

Typical fees for whelping boxes range from $35 for a small one to $65 for a large one. Breeders tend to have very individual needs without a large variety to choose from commercially. One popular telescoping dog ramp sells for $99 while others for large dogs go up to $255. Custom-made cat condos sell for $100 to $300 or more. Check out the prices people are willing to pay on eBay and then add more for local delivery.

Equipment Needed

You'll need lumber, supplies and tools depending on the materials you use. You can buy plans for doghouses and cat condos and then add individual touches. Many products also require cushions or upholstery so it helps if you have some experience there as well. If you need to hone your skills, see if a nearby Home Depot has any applicable courses or how-to books/videos.

101 Home based Businesses for Pet Lovers

Getting Started

Contact local breeders or pet club officers and ask them what kind of products they would like to be able to buy. Offer to make some products for the local animal shelter in exchange for the rights to advertise that they have your product.

Make a few items for your own or friend's pets and create a three-ring photo album of your work and some flyers of the more typical products (whelping boxes, ramps, etc).

Distribute your flyers at pet shows, breeders and kennels, veterinarians and pet or feed stores, depending on the type of products you're willing to make.

If you live near an upscale, new development, leave flyers or doorknob hangars and try a small classified ad in a local newspaper. Many new homeowners would like to customize an area for their pet and you can take your photo album of samples to call on them.

Pitfalls to Avoid

Don't use expensive lumber. The pets can't tell the difference and as long it's strong enough, there's no reason not to use seconds or scraps.

If you're building something that attaches to or changes a home structure, there may be building codes that apply to the work. Check with the local licensing or zoning offices to make certain you do not inadvertently violate a building code.

Growth Potential & Expansion

The more ingenious you can be in solving a pet's problems or making them more comfortable in their home, the more referrals you'll get from satisfied pet owners.

PET CARPENTRY

If you develop a product that proves popular, take it around to local pet stores to see if they'll carry it on consignment.

Competition

What carpenters do you know who specialize in pet carpentry?

Keys to Success

Your biggest hurdle will be in marketing your service. As soon as you do an unusual custom job, take good quality photos and send news releases to all your local print and electronic media.

Resources

How To Start a Homebased Carpentry Business,
2nd Edition by Charles Self
(Globe Pequot Press, 1997, 240-pages)
$24.99 at www.amazon.com

For an example of a dog owner who made a ramp herself using her own plans: `http://www.bouviers.net/info/dogramp.html`

For cat lovers: CreateACatCondo.com
http://www.createacatcondo.com/
1847 South Main Street
Gainesville, FL 32601
E-mail to molly@createacatcondo.com

For examples of products, visit Sears Craftsman website:
`http://www.sears.com/sr/craftsman/projects_tips/weekend_warrior/pt_ww_trophycase.jsp`

67 Pet Carry All

General Concept

Similar to baby diaper bag's, you create custom tote bags that can transport all your pet's supplies when you two travel. The bags should be moisture resistant and easily cleaned.

What makes this work is having either a clever or custom design on the bag. Many pet owners would enjoy having a bag with a photo of Fluffy or Fido on it. Heavy canvas bags with a plastic lining are ideal for this.

If you can sew, you can create unique bags with unique price tags. If you can't sew, buy canvas totes and add cover designs and inside linings.

Profit Potential

Designer diaper bags can sell for up to $80. Canine and feline version usually retail for $20 to $60. One popular tote, the small Sherpa Tote Around Town Bag sells for $54.99 and is 12" w x 7" D x 15" H. The more personalized the design, the more you can charge for it.

Equipment Needed

If you make your own, you'll need a sewing machine. You can buy patterns for totes (such as diaper bags) or create your own. If you can embroider or cross stitch, either makes an attractive cover for these carryalls. You also can screen print photos of pets for covers. Depending on your design, you may need some other materials. You may prefer to find a wholesaler for basic canvas totes and add on to them with your own designs. If you don't sew, use glue.

Getting Started

Buy the cheapest similar type of bag you can find and reverse engineer it. Understand the shape and design. Typically all that changes on a tote is the fabric and cover design. When you understand the shape and have developed a design, visit a fabric or crafts shop and decide what kind of material you want to use for the cover. It's nice to have a zippered closing and you'll want sturdy handles (preferably leather).

See if local pet shops will sell your bags on consignment. If you find a design that sells well, you can try small classified ads in publications targeted for the type of pet on the cover of your carryall. If you have several made, try selling them at a local flea market or craft show. You can see which designs attract viewers and buyers.

Pitfalls to Avoid

Don't violate any copyrights if you use photographs or clip art for your designs. Use original designs, photographs of your customer's pet or hire an artist to design something but make sure you have a written agreement with the artist stating that this is a work-for-hire and you own all rights to it.

Growth Potential & Expansion

Offer several sizes: small for a day at the park, medium for a weekend trip and large for a week's travel.

Offer other shapes than the standard tote. Try a cylindrical shape with a drawstring closing and round flat bottom.

101 Home based Businesses for Pet Lovers

Sell to other pet businesses. For instance, a pet store or pet grooming shop may buy bags with their logo and contact information on them. Other potential clients include veterinarians, day care facilities, stables, pet bakeries and feed stores. If your product becomes popular, you can show it at pet product trade shows and wholesale to retail and Internet pet supply stores.

Competition

It's amazing how many pet owners collect everything with their pet or a particular breed on it. Try to identify popular breeds; e.g., Maltese or Bengal cat or sun conure (bird), that have devoted owners ready to add to their collections of pet-theme products.

Keys to Success

Include a zippered pocket on the inside to hold the owner's car keys and wallet.

Make sure the opening can be secured so everything doesn't fall out if the owner happens to drop the bag while trying to grab onto an errant leash.

Resources

Examples of similar products:
Triptych Gifts and Home Decor
http://www.triptychonline.com

68 Pet Cemetery

General Concept

You provide a cemetery for pet owners to bury and memorialize their beloved pets. This is ideal if you own sufficient property and your state and local laws permit a pet cemetery.

Pets can be buried in a private plot or in a communal plot. In a private burial, a pet's remains are prepared separately and placed in an individual gravesite, crypt, or mausoleum. In a common or communal burial, a pet's remains are buried in the same plot with other deceased pets.

Profit Potential

There are more than 600 active Pet Cemeteries in the United States. Of these, about 400 are operating businesses.

Getting Started

Many pet cemeteries operate in conjunction with other pet related business: boarding kennels, grooming salons, training centers and veterinarian hospitals. These businesses may want to joint venture with you to create a cemetery.

Try to establish relationships with local veterinarians and leave your business card or brochures at their offices. Pets left at clinics or hospitals may be sent to the local land fill or rendering plants. The final decision belongs to the pet owner. Make sure your marketing materials alert owners to these facts and the alternative you offer.

Make arrangements for cremation services with a veterinarian that does this or through an existing human funeral home in your area. It can be expensive to establish one of these yourself. You are better off having a joint venture with a business that knows how to do this and already comply with all state and local laws. Just ensure that each animal is individually cremated so you get the right pet's ashes.

Pitfalls to Avoid

Local or County ordinances determine where a pet can be buried. These laws are set up mainly due to the health hazards caused by other animals trying to dig them up. Make sure you check this out.

You will need a business license and insurance. An umbrella policy should cover you for liability issues as well as potential damage to an urn or memorial.

You should own the land rather than lease it, and the cemetery's property deed should state that the land will always remain a pet cemetery regardless of ownership. You must think about what happens when you pass on and have a legally existing arrangement so that your pet cemetery can continue in business whether you are present or not.

Growth Potential & Expansion

Establish a care fund (as do human cemeteries) to insure that funds will be available for the continuing maintenance of the grounds and roadways so that owners pay an annual or one-time fee for this service.

Sell caskets, headstones and urns. Offer graveside services. Wholesale prices of small pet caskets run $100 to $300. Urns are about $50.

Pet Cemetery

If you want to acquire your own crematory, there are two types of crematoriums used: a hearth (or oven), or an incinerator/grate. Bear in mind that you will have to conform to stringent environmental laws if you operate a crematory. Before you invest several thousand dollars in buying and setting up one, make sure you could recover your costs.

Resources

International Association of Pet Cemeteries
http://www.iaopc.com/memberapp.htm
P.O. Box 163
5055 Route 11
Ellenburg Depot, NY 12935
Phone: 518.594.3000

The largest manufacturer of pet caskets is Hoegh Pet Caskets
http://www.tspetmemorials.com/caskets2.html
T&S Pet Memorials
P.O. Box 5173
Ocean Isle Beach, NC 28469
Phone: 910.575.2943

Everlasting Stone Monuments
http://www.everlastingstone.com
P.O. Box 995-TR
Barre, VT 05641-0995

Phone: 802.454.1050

69 Pet Club of the Month

General Concept

This isn't a new pet every month! It is a subscription service where you provide a new product for the pet every month. For example, current clubs offer treats, bandanas, collars and even a pet-health kit with vitamins and supplements for reptiles. Think how convenient it would be for the busy snake owner to get a month's supply of the products (except for live feed!) he needs to take care of and amuse his pet.

Profit Potential

Treats usually run $10 to $12 per month. Collars or bandanas typically run $8-10 per month or more depending on size. All pet clubs require at least a three-month membership. If you offer more exotic items (see www.RhinestoneDogCollars.net), you can charge more.

You must require at least a three-month membership to make this worthwhile for the customer and for you. Do roll shipping into the monthly fee so people don't feel you're trying to nickel and dime them.

Be explicit in your marketing materials and website whether you handle international members which (from the U.S.) includes Mexico and Canada. If you can charge enough and use the U.S. Postal Service to do your shipments (because they offer free guidance and help on the laws), you may want to include these two countries. Europe and beyond may be prohibitively expensive due to postage and tariffs.

Pet Club of the Month

Equipment Needed

You need a re-sellers certificate from your state. You need a source of supplies, or you must make your own.

You need the normal computer set up with Internet access and telephone voice mail or answering service. You also need software that can handle the subscription process and show products attractively.

You need a recurring credit card billing process. Customers sign up and pay for the first month, and then are automatically billed each month until they cancel. You can do this with your own merchant credit card account or use a third party service such as http://www.PayPal.com or http://www.iBill.com.

Getting Started

Find a product or develop a kit, such as the health care kit for snakes, that isn't readily available at pet stores and that would appeal to both the pet and the owner.

Create a website to advertise your product.

Send flyers to pet clubs and press releases to local and industry news media.

Pitfalls to Avoid

Do not ship food or live animals, including insects, unless you've done your homework regarding the laws. If you want to sell treats, buy them from a commercial pet bakery so you get them already packaged.

Growth Potential & Expansion

You can expand the types of products you offer and the types of pets you service. There isn't a large club of the month for horse owners and enthusiastics, but there are plenty of those people out there.

Competition

This is a young industry for pets although the dog market has many pet clubs. Instead, try a bird-toy-of-the-month club.

Keys to Success

People won't remain members if you just offer the same products they can buy at PetsMart or Petco. You should own or have experience with the pet that's the subject of your club.

Resources

For examples:
Canine Cookie Company
http://www.canine-cookie.com/month.htm
21527 Paine Ave.
Lago Vista, TX 78645

Moon Valley Collars Collar Club
http://www.moonvalleycollars.com/club.html
PO Box 802 - Sonoma, CA 95476
Phone: 707.935.1449

For subscription website software:
VisionGate
http://www.visiongateportal.com

aMember
http://membership.cgi-central.net/scripts/amember/

MemberGate (top of the line but expensive)
http://www.membergate.com/

70 Pet Detective

General Concept

Always dreamed of being a P.I. and love pets? Here's your dream combination, the pet detective. You locate missing, stolen or lost pets.

Profit Potential

Don't expect to get rich but this may be an enjoyable second income for some. Fees typically start at $75.

Equipment Needed

Flashlight, good walking shoes or boots, muzzles and collars. Get a vest in international orange with your logo or business name embroidered on it.

You'll need to create flyers of lost pets. Either buy a scanner and computer with printer or have it done at Kinkos or other store. Always charge the client actual expenses.

Getting Started

Distribute flyers or business cards at vets, pet stores, groomers, and animal shelters. Try a classified ad in a small, local newspaper like Thrifty Nickel that are delivered free to the area you want to serve.

Pitfalls to Avoid

You must be in good health. This job requires a lot of walking and crawling under homes or other structures. Get a tetanus shot before you start your business and make sure you have health insurance. Bites and scratches are part of the business. Be sure to get a tetanus shot before you start.

Don't guarantee to find a pet and don't charge contingent on finding a pet. Charge for your time and expertise using a daily rate ($150). Get agreement with the client up front how long you will work on the case.

Growth Potential & Expansion

Teach other people how to become pet detectives including offering this course at local community colleges and sell a booklet you write that tells people how to go about finding their lost pet.

Competition

Minimal.

Keys to Success

Charge enough. You can't be a charity and a business at the same time. You need to charge enough to make this worthwhile.

Most states license and regulate who can call themselves a detective. These laws rarely apply to pet detectives, however, it would be wise to check with your state licensing agency to ensure you can operate with "detective" in your name.

Resources

Examples of this business:
http://www.lostpetfoundpet.com/Get%20help.htm
http://www.sherlockbones.com/

71 Pet Food Delivery

General Concept

You deliver premium pet food on a regular basis to pet owners in upscale and retirement communities. You buy from a wholesaler and always provide fresh pet food.

Profit Potential

Charge on a weekly or monthly basis. You'll run yourself ragged doing this on an on-demand basis. At least require 24-hours notice before scheduling a delivery and have a minimum fee (usually $15 to $25).

Equipment Needed

Dependable vehicle, pickup truck or van works best, with substantial liability insurance because you're using it for business purposes. Resellers permit from your Secretary of State's office so you can buy from wholesalers and not pay a sales tax.

Liability insurance for your vehicle and for yourself because you're driving so much for business could be thousands of dollars a year depending on where you live. Shop around for rates.

Getting Started

Get your business license and start handing out flyers or brochures at veterinarian offices, active retirement areas (e.g., Del Webb Sun Cities) and condominium/apartment offices.

Be sure all marketing materials state which geographical areas you service (by zip code or name) and include a price schedule.

This pre-screens clients and doesn't annoy those who don't want to be bothered having to call to get prices.

Pitfalls to Avoid

Don't service too large a geographic area. You'll waste time traveling and spend too much in vehicle expenses. Look for upscale communities with many homes or condominiums in a contained area.

There's more money to be made by selling your own brand or being a distributor for just one brand of dog food, but there's more potential for liability issues as well. The Food and Drug Administration recently warned one franchise company that it might have provided Canadian dog food made from beef contaminated with Mad Cow disease. It would be very difficult to recover your customer base if this happened to you even though you did nothing wrong.

If you're not a distributor or manufacturer, make sure your invoices note that you are acting as a delivery service only and do not control or guarantee the quality of the food. It's recommended that you have a local lawyer review a paragraph to this effect that you can add on your invoices and marketing materials.

Growth Potential & Expansion

Sell water containers and pet bowls, both designer and electronic self-feeding types, for extra money.

Competition

Depends on your area. Target upscale senior citizen areas where the pet owners don't want to or can't lug 25-pound dog food bags.

Pet Food Delivery

Keys to Success

Distribute door hangers in the upscale area(s) you want to service. Repackage dog food if you have to so you aren't leaving a heavy bag with a senior citizen. Five or 10-pound bags will help sell your service. Offer to unpack and put away the bags or cans for the pet owner.

Resources

Examples of this business:
http://www.paulspetfood.com
http://www.gooberexpress.com/
http://www.petfoodservices.com/services.htm

72 Pet Gift Baskets

General Concept

You combine multi-media products related to one theme into a gift basket (don't take "basket" too literally). For instance, develop a gift basket for owners of a new Yorkshire Terrier puppy. Include a book about Yorkies or training a puppy, a couple of toys suitable for tiny puppies, an audio or video tape on housebreaking and a collectible (coffee cup, wall plaque, notepads, etc) that has a Yorkie picture or screen print on them.

Profit Potential

One website devoted to dogs offers two puppy gift baskets: one is a stripped down version in a designer paper bag for $19.95 while the other is a full kit in a carrying case for $54.95.

A website offering cat gift baskets sells one type for $36.95 which includes collar, toys, treats, and a catnip pillow while a website offering horse gift baskets has a basic package for $29.95.

Do mark up everything and cover your labor in your price; however, do not get carried away. It's very difficult to sell a $75 gift basket to individual consumers.

Equipment Needed

What do you want to hold your gift items? If your gift "baskets" are small enough, you'll need a shrink-wrap machine (about $200). Whatever the size, you'll need bubble wrap and shipping/packaging materials. Take a look at http://www.quill.com for supplies and check out the auctions at eBay.

Pet Gift Baskets

Getting Started

Get a resellers permit from your state so you can buy wholesale.

Decide on your market and your theme. Build a couple of gift baskets and take photos of them. Take your baskets to craft and street fairs and see what themes and products attract the most attention.

Create flyers with your photos and distribute to local pet stores, veterinarian offices, animal breeders, feed stores, and animal shows.

Send your vet a free gift basket with your business card prominently displayed. Offer baskets to large, prominent charitable auctions and raffle sales. Develop a website for your products and/or sell them on eBay or Yahoo stores. Get listed in Google's Froogle at `http://froogle.google.com/`.

Pitfalls to Avoid

Don't spend too much on supplies. Visit gift shows, Costco and Sam's Club, eBay and the Internet for reasonable suppliers and supplies.

If you ship, have your customer pay for postage plus enough to cover packaging supplies and your labor to pack and ship. Include enough to cover insurance at no obvious additional cost. Some customers will want to delete insurance if you offer it as a separate cost (these are the customers certain to receive damaged baskets or have them lost in the mail).

There are many laws, local and federal, related to shipping live plants and foods such as fruits. If you use foods in your basket, make them pre-packaged ones that you've bought from a supplier who has a commercial kitchen.

Avoid products that go out of date such as calendars or are too trendy such as a photo of the current U.S. President or momentary TV star. Buy in bulk only those items that remain evergreen (such as coffee cups with a pet photo) and have a place to store them.

Growth Potential & Expansion

Team with a local pet professional and offer discounts if they buy your basket for their clients, such as a pet groomer who sends one to her best customers at Christmas. It's easier and more lucrative to sell to businesses rather than individual customers.

Competition

There's a lot of competition. You need to target niches and market relentlessly. With all the general dog and cat products, why not appeal to reptile owners or a specific breed of dog or cat.

Keys to Success

Your creativity and marketing make you succeed or fail.

Resources

Examples:
For dogs—O! You Lucky Dog! at
http://www.homestead.com/oyouluckydog/
For horses—NickerBaskets at
http://www.nickerbaskets.com/
Gift Basket Review magazine ($29.95 subscription)
815 Haines Street
Jacksonville, FL 32206
Phone: 800.729.6338

Gift Basket Business.com (good resource with links to suppliers)
http://www.giftbasketbusiness.com/

73 Pet Humor Website

General Concept

You operate a web portal for your favorite type of pet with the emphasis on humor. Links will be to websites that specialize in humor or offer humorous items, such as cartoons of a dog breed. You can use a broader type of pet such as "dogs" or specialize such as "Bulldogs."

Profit Potential

Income for the website will come from affiliate sales from your website. You also may start a fee-charging weekly or monthly e-mail service with a joke of the day or humorous story. There's a reason Jay Leno and Dave Letterman can make so much money. It's tough to be funny and to do it day in and day out.

Find a specialization that isn't covered well. Dogs have many, many individual websites. Look at certain breeds of dogs.

Have a creative, unique voice. Many of the existing websites don't have loyal followings because they're so broad with no overarching themes or unifying features.

Equipment Needed

Website and reliable ISP.

Software to create and maintain a website. Dreamweaver MX and Fireworks MX are the gold standard but there are less expensive options such as Microsoft FrontPage.

Material for your website. Set up a discussion board so website visitors can leave funny stories about their pets. Canvass

Pet Humor Website

copyright-free material (usually from the 1920s and earlier) for material you can modernize and then reprint.

Getting Started

Create your website. Then take three paths.

One, join affiliate programs that make sense for your website but do use LinkShare `http://www.linkshare.com/` and/or Commission Junction at `http://www.cj.com/` in addition to any individual sites such as Amazon.com that offer affiliate programs.

Two, get your website ranked as high as possible in Google and the other web search sites. Do not use a software program; submit your website individually to the major search sites.

Three, trade links (but not indiscriminately) with good websites that relate to your type of pet. Approach the webmasters with an individual e-mail asking to trade links. Do NOT use a link farm as search engines may penalize you for it.

Pitfalls to Avoid

Do NOT violate any copyrights. You can't use a joke simply because you heard it on TV. If you like something you hear from a comedian, change it enough to make it useable.

Don't violate search engine rules. Visit Google, Lycos and the other search engines. All offer rules and information about how to submit sites and what they forbid.

Growth Potential & Expansion

Joint venture with products or professionals related to your pet. A major business may be willing to team with you to offer prizes for "Pet Hero of the Month" or some other competition that you sponsor on your website.

Start a small, print publication sold through mail subscriptions. For instance, a monthly two-sided letterhead size "newsletter" with humorous stories would be welcome at many retirement and convalescence care facilities where the residents are not computer users. If the publication becomes popular, sell advertising for it.

Competition

There are many websites doing this for the more popular pets (e.g., dogs) but no major players. Few of the websites have any personality.

Keys to Success

Good material and high ranking in the search engines are the components for success.

Once you've been running and have perfected your website, consider using Google ad words at `https://adwords.google.com` or Overture at `http://www.content.overture.com/d/home/`

Resources

Examples:
Good Dog Humor
`http://www.workingdogweb.com/cartoons.htm`
EquiSearch
`http://www.equisearch.com/humor/`
Cat Humor
`http://www.nanceestar.com/CatHumor.html`

74 Pet Insurance

General Concept

You help pet owners find the best insurance for their pets. This can be as an independent insurance agent/broker using offline or online marketing to reach clients. Pet insurance covers veterinary fees and animal hospital expenses. Policy terms vary widely.

An alternative is to operate a website that compares and explains pet insurance policies. Make money through advertising and affiliate sales. Don't limit yourself to just insurance. If (say you specialize in horses), someone will buy equine insurance, what other horse-related products and services might you include on your website? Visit Commission Junction at www.cj.com and LinkShare at http://www.linkshare.com/ to compare and enroll in affiliate programs.

Profit Potential

Although selling insurance offers the potential for high incomes, few do well, as it requires discipline and a thick skin to sell anything. The average annual premium for pet insurance is $200 per animal.

The majority of your clients are likely to be dog owners. Why dogs? They are the most popular pet and the ones that have the most genetic diseases and injuries. There is a wide open market here as the American Animal Hospital Association estimates only 1% of the 38-million dog owners in the U.S. carry pet insurance.

Equipment Needed

If you want to be an insurance agent or broker, you'll need a license from your state. Usually pet insurance is a "Property and Casualty" class of business and requires some period of study plus passing an examination. Check with your state's Insurance Commission.

Getting Started

Get licensed as an insurance agent. It's helpful to have this even if you intend to only offer advice via website. You'll be forced to understand policy terms in order to pass the state examination.

Make up flyers or brochures and leave them at pet businesses such as feed and pet stores, veterinarian offices, groomers and stables or kennels. Offer to give presentations at community groups on why you should have and how to find good pet insurance coverage.

Pitfalls to Avoid

Do not sell insurance policies online without guidance from a lawyer who knows the insurance industry. It would be easy to unknowingly break a state law not to mention the myriad federal laws that apply. If you're a licensed, registered agent for a company that helps you create websites, that's fine but don't attempt to sell online without legal advice.

Growth Potential & Expansion

Get corporate accounts. Target small to medium businesses in your areas and develop group policies the companies can offer to their employees. The big insurance companies already market to large companies.

Pet Insurance

Joint venture with breeders to offer a package deal when someone buys a pet. Offer insurance policies for other coverage.

After all, you're licensed to sell casualty and property coverage so why not offer it? It's becoming increasingly difficult for homeowners with large dogs or certain breeds (e.g., pit bulls) to obtain homeowner's coverage.

Competition

Many sites rank insurance policies but few target pet owners exclusively.

Keys to Success

As an insurance agent or broker, you must be willing to sell and that requires face-to-face contact.

If you're the shy type, concentrate on offering information and product comparisons over the Internet.

101 Home based Businesses for Pet Lovers

Resources

Example of a website that rates pet insurance policies:
Money Supermarket
http://www.moneysupermarket.com/GeneralInsurance/

PetHealth Inc.
(looking for agents/brokers)
http://www.petcareinsurance.com/brokers/faq.asp

The American Kennel Club offers policies through
Pet Partners, Inc.
http://www.akc.org/vetoutreach/headlinenews_16.cfm

Veterinary Pet Insurance (U.S.
largest company but has its own representatives.
It does, however, offer affiliate programs.)
http://www.petinsurance.com/

As an example of the range of insurance coverage available, visit Unique Coverage Insurance at
http://www.americaninsurancedepot.com/misc.htm

75 Pet Party Planner

General Concept

For the pet who has everything, offer to create and host party events. Host at your home (if your local ordinances and zoning permit), at the pet owner's home or at a business that co-sponsors the party.

Profit Potential

One company in Hawaii offers luas with doggy leis ($3 per dog) and doggie-treat bags ($4 per dog) with a $20 (10 portions) doggy-safe cake. Celebrate events such as birthdays, obedience school graduations or release from quarantine.

Don't rely on a service charge alone (i.e., $X per party), sell the favors, etc. that create the party with a mark-up. You won't get rich but you can have fun and earn a part-time income.

Equipment Needed

Your creativity. Buy supplies on an as-needed basis.

Getting Started

Get licensed by your city and state and make sure your auto insurance policy will cover the use of your car for your business.

Get a reseller's permit from your state so you can buy wholesale. Develop a relationship with a pet bakery to supply you treats at wholesale and see if they will co-sponsor party events at their store.

Leave marketing materials at veterinarians, obedience schools, groomers, and local pet stores. Try to joint venture with dog trainers and community colleges that offer dog training or puppy kindergarten classes. They may sponsor graduation day parties.

Pitfalls to Avoid

Don't serve too large an area so you aren't wasting too much time traveling and buying gasoline. Target an upscale zip code area.

Don't waste time trying this on solitary, independent pets like cats. Target dogs first and then expand to other species if someone requests it.

Growth Potential & Expansion

Offer pet taxi services as an add-on.

Competition

Minimal if at all.

Keys to Success

Referrals from satisfied customers.

Resources

Examples:
http://www.roversplacedogdaycare.com/otherservices.htm
http://www.pawtytime.com/pawties.htm

76 Pet Photographer

General Concept

Take photographs, including digital photos of people's pets. Use costumes and themes to add appeal.

Profit Potential

Check local prices of local competition but aim to sell package deals of several photos at least for $200.

Equipment Needed

Professional camera (35mm) and lighting. Either make prints yourself or subcontract with a larger facility. Also have a digital camera for electronic photos and a computer with color printer.

Make sure you are current on new equipment and techniques. Community colleges offer inexpensive courses. If you lack the basic equipment, you can spend up to $5,000 getting it all.

Trim costs by renting equipment or buying discontinued models.

You'll need a studio or one you can rent periodically. Take photos at a client's home or in public places like dog parks as much as possible.

Getting Started

Volunteer to do photos for animal shelters and at pet fairs. Leave coupons for a discount on photos for shelters and pet stores to give to people who buy new pets. Hand out cards or brochures at every local pet show.

Joint venture with other pet businesses such as groomers, veterinarians, doggy day cares, pet stores to offer joint packages (photo plus grooming session) at a fixed rate. If they won't joint venture, see if they'll hand out your coupon to every customer.

Pitfalls to Avoid

Charge enough. Expect to use many more rolls of film to get a good pet shot than you do for a human. Don't forget processing and print costs.

Competition

Check your local phonebook. You shouldn't have too much competition yet.

Growth Potential & Expansion

Take stock photographs that you sell to advertising agencies, clip art outfits and other media.

Add pet photos to just about anything from computer mouse pads to T-shirts for additional income.

Target the exotic pet market (go to their shows) as you won't have as much competition here.

Two sidelines to consider (more equipment required): 1) restore photos digitally or 2) copy photos for people who've lost negatives. See `http://www.photographic.com` for details.

Keys to Success

Patience and a love of animals. If you become upset or impatient with an animal, it will sense it and become even more difficult.

Resources

Rohn Engh's Photosource International
http://www.photosource.com

Professional Photographers of America, Inc.,
229 Peachtree St. NE, Suite 2200
Atlanta, GA 30303
Phone: 404.522.8600
http://www.ppa.com/

For articles and how-to information:
Kodak Company
http://www.kodak.com

Photographic Magazine (worth a subscription)
http://www.photographic.com/

77 Pet Registration

General Concept

Losing a beloved pet is a horrible experience. You can lessen the pain by offering a local pet registration service to help locate missing pets. This service allows pet owners to leave photos and information (such as tattoos or microchips) about the pet with your service. You contact animal shelters and respond to ads about found pets to try to reunite a missing pet with his owner.

Profit Potential

Offer two or three rates for registration packages depending on the degree of service the pet owner wants. Some owners, who travel a great deal, may want you to take responsibility for everything related to finding their pets. Others may just want you to have photos and information on the pet so if they happen to be out-of-town or unavailable when their pet goes missing, you are able to try to track down the pet. Registration packages usually start at $45 a year.

Equipment Needed

Computer with a database software program to keep track of all your clients. Camera, preferably a digital camera, for taking pet photos.

Getting Started

Most pet registration is aimed at dogs and sometimes cats. There is an open market for other types of pets who are likely

Pet Registration

to get away including horses, rodents and reptiles. If you handle exotic pets, send out press releases to local media on your unusual business.

Leave your flyers or brochures at dog/cat shows, veterinarian offices, local animal shelters, pet boarding facilities, groomers and pet supply stores. Don't overlook your wide rural market. There are plenty of feed stores catering to horses and other valuable animals outside the urban center.

Any owner with an expensive show or stud animal is a candidate for your service.

Pitfalls to Avoid

NEVER microchip or tattoo a pet yourself. In most states, there are strict laws about the training an individual needs to perform such services. You are just the registration service. This also reduces your potential for liability.

Growth Potential & Expansion

This is a natural extension of a pet detective, pet tatttoo or electronic (invisible) fencing service. If you don't already run one of those, joint venture with one.

An easy-to-run add on is to offer reminder services to owners for such things as vaccination schedules or pet birthdays. You can do this via e-mail or telephone.

You also might team with a local service organization and offer this service as a fundraiser for them. The organization would get $x from each registration they provide you. Remember, your contribution would be tax deductible.

Competition

Your local competition, if any, is likely to be a private or government-run animal shelter. Marketing and personalized service will be the key to your success.

Again, do not try to microchip or tattoo yourself.

There is keen competition for those services, and it would be difficult to compete against national registries such as the American Kennel Club's for dog microchips. Your market is your local area, and you provide services beyond a mere phone list tied to a microchip.

Keys to Success

Keep up-to-date with the latest in identification devices and equipment to find lost pets, such as global positioning units, which will soon offer microchips for dog collars. Joint venture with a local distributor once they're ready for release.

Submit every successful reunion of pet and owner to your local media.

Contact your clients each year to update their information and to renew their registration.

Pet Registration

Resources

For an example of a business doing this:
Petigree International Pet Registry, LLC
http://www.petigree.org/serv.html

For manufacturer products for other than dogs and cats -
Electronic ID, Inc.
http://www.electronicidinc.com/
3573 S. Nolan River Road
Cleburne, TX 76033 USA
Phone: 817.517.7190
You might team with their local distributor to offer the registration service.

78 Pet Referral Service

General Concept

You locate reputable cat or dog breeders for individuals who want to buy a pet but don't have the knowledge or time themselves to screen breeders. As crossbreeding for specific qualities becomes more popular, this service can be expected to increase in popularity among affluent would-be dog owners.

Rather than take a percentage of the sales price from the breeder, it is better to charge the would-be dog or cat owner for your service. That prevents a conflict of interest and allows you to screen out breeders who don't meet your standards. It also makes it easier to get paid.

Decide if you will provide this service via e-mail/phone or insist on a personal visit with the client.

Profit Potential

Fees typically start at $100. Remember a rare purebred pet can sell for up to $1,500.

Equipment Needed

Not much. A computer with e-mail and Internet access, a phone with voice mail, and a great database program or Rolodex with names and information about many, many breeders.

Marketing materials are crucial as most people will not be aware that such a service even exists.

Printing will be your biggest expense when you're starting.

Pet Referral Service

Getting Started

Develop a form for your potential clients. It should indicate the breed, gender, color, any special characteristics that the client wants. Get as much information about the client's lifestyle as possible so you can guide him/her to select a pet that will fit well with his life. Use the form as a service agreement and have the client sign it. This clarifies what you were supposed to do.

Distribute flyers or business cards at vets, pet stores, groomers, and dog or cat shows. Advertise in your local newspaper Sunday classified in the Pets for Sale section. Purchase a show catalog which lists the names and addresses of breeders and send them your business cards or flyers with a sheet for them to fill out and send back to you (provide an envelope with return postage). You'll want to know about breeding stock, awards, certifications, what genetic testing the breeder does and ask for references from veterinarian and former customers. Offer a money-back guarantee if you can't locate a breeder of a pet the buyer is seeking. That should be your only money-back guarantee.

Pitfalls to Avoid

Most states regulate the sale of animals. Never handle the animal yourself. That introduces legal complications. You are a referral service and that's it. Don't even offer to pick up or transport the pet.

Have the breeder call the client if s/he has a dog or cat for sale that meets your client's needs. The breeder then can make his/her own decision whether to sell to this person.

Never handle a disreputable breeder even if they have a popular breed of dog.

101 Home based Businesses for Pet Lovers

Make sure your breeder is listed in the American Kennel Club's Referral Search and a member of his breed club. All the breed clubs have Codes of Ethics and usually will drum out breeders that fail to meet these codes.

Growth Potential & Expansion

Create online or written forms that help clients determine what breed is best for them and sell this whether people use your service or not. If you make this a success, you can document how and what you do and sell it to other people as a how-to course on opening their own pet referral business.

Competition

Minimal.

Keys to Success

Charge enough and don't do business with disreputable breeders.

Always do a follow-up with your clients and find out if they were satisfied with the breeder and got the pet they wanted. Send out stamped, self-addressed postcards or envelopes for your clients to use. You must know which breeders are doing a good job for you and which ones you should put in the do-not-call category.

Resources

American Kennel Club Breeder's Referral
http://www.akc.org/breeds/breederinfo/breeder_search.cfm
260 Madison Ave
NYC, NY 10016
Phone: 212.696.8200

79 Pet Sitting

General Concept

You take care of critters while their owners are away, either at work or on vacation. Usually includes taking in the mail, etc to make the home look lived in.

Profit Potential

Visits usually run $10 to $25 for a 30-40 minute visit. Pet Sitters International survey showed annual incomes of $15,000 to $125,000 (if you have help).

Equipment Needed

Nothing much—depending on the animals you handle, extra leash, flashlight, pet treats, leather gloves (for a pet who doesn't like being held) and cleanup supplies.

Bonding and liability insurance (plan on at least $200) that is cheapest by joining one of the organizations in Resources and getting group rates. After that, it's just how much you want to spend on marketing tools.

Getting Started

Get your business license and start handing out flyers or brochures at veterinarian offices, pet stores and condominium/apartment offices.

Be sure all marketing materials state which geographical areas you service (by zip code or name) and include a price schedule. This pre-screens clients and doesn't eliminate those who won't be bothered having to call to get prices.

Pitfalls to Avoid

Don't service too large a geographic area. You'll waste time traveling and spend too much in car expenses.

Don't lose client keys—keep them attached to your body with key rings on a belt or wrist bracelet.

Growth Potential & Expansion

Add employees or independent contractors. Become an agent for other pet sitters and take a percentage of their charges. Sell animal products.

The fastest way to join the $100,000 a year club is to copy the house-cleaning companies. Use two person teams for each visit. One person plays with the pet while the other does cleanup/house-sitting services. This can cut your visit time in half and allow you to do more jobs in a day.

Competition

Lots. This is an easy business to start. Consider specializing in types of animals. For example, specialize in cats, snakes and reptiles, or birds.

Good word of mouth is the best way to get new clients.

Keys to Success

Love the animals you take care of and be dependable. Never, ever discuss a client, a client's home or other information about the client or his pet in public. You never know who could be listening; such as a burglar who's delighted to find out that the Smith's are in Europe for two months.

Show up when scheduled and follow the client's directions to the letter.

Pet Sitting

Specialize in the rarer forms of pets (not just dogs or cats) such as horses or reptiles.

Resources

Pet Sitters International,
http://www.petsit.com/
201 East King Street
King, NC 27021-9161
Phone: 336.983.9222

National Association of Professional Pet Sitters
http://www.napps.com
6 State Road #113
Mechanicsburg, PA 17050
Phone: 717.691.5565

How to Start a Pet Sitting Business
(and What to Do
Once You Have)
available at
http://www.toybreeds.com

Sample websites:
http://www.catsmeowpetsitting.com/home.html
http://www.creaturecomfortscorp.com/

Pet Care Agreement from www.nolo.com
(a great resource for all legal issues)
http://www.nolo.com/lawstore/products/product.cfm
/objectID/ADBA6762-604B-4BFA-9DDB22507CADA87A
Available as download for $8

80 PET STATIONERY

General Concept

You sell customized stationery to pet owners and people with pet businesses. For instance, many dog breeders want their dog breed on everything. If the breeder uses a mail order or Internet supplier, however, every breeder of Maltese dogs is likely to have the same image of a Maltese on their letterhead.

Instead, you get photos of the individual's dog (or other pet), scan it in and create a letterhead. Then have a local printer print the papers and envelopes for your customer.

Profit Potential

Quality papers only with printing typically sell for around $50 for a box of 50 letterhead with matching envelopes. You can charge more if you add photographs to the letterhead.

Equipment Needed

Digital camera ($300) if you want to take photographs of pets and software to reverse, tone and size the image. You can go for a high-end product like Adobe Photoshop but a cheaper product such as Microsoft Picture It ($70) will do just fine.

If you don't want to take photos yourself, arrange to send business to a local pet photographer in exchange for a fee for each customer.

Getting Started

Find a local printer who does quality work and is willing to take on your business. You may buy the product from the printer and sell it (with mark-up) to your customer or act as a broker for the printer and get your fee from him (usually less remunerative).

Develop a sample book in conjunction with the printer. Your sample book can be a three-ring binder with clear page protectors to hold the samples. Use photos of your own pet to create letterhead, note cards, and envelopes or whatever personalized papers the printer can handle. Use different colors and types of papers so customers can easily visualize how their stationery might look.

Take your sample book around to pet businesses, such as breeders, groomers and trainers, who might want personalized stationery for marketing purposes. Attend pet shows and offer your products to the proud owners. If the price is reasonable, get a booth at your area's largest pet show and take orders there.

Pitfalls to Avoid

You need good photos to make good stationery. Learn how to use a digital camera and the photo enhancing software so you can take photographs (and charge extra) when the customer is unable to produce a quality photo.

The other major problem is misspelled names, addresses and words. Triple check to ensure you have no errors and always have the customer check and initial a mock-up (single-copy example on inexpensive laser paper) before you print it.

Growth Potential & Expansion

Nothing prevents you from expanding beyond pets to offer stationery with people's homes, business storefronts or other hobbies on it.

Also offer line drawings of pets in lieu of photos. Some people prefer a black-and-white or sepia tinted stationery reminiscent of the Victorian era.

If you're talented or can hire someone who is, develop a cartoon pet-image that might appeal to businesses that don't want to feature any one pet.

Competition

There are mail order houses that provide this—at varying prices and varying quality. Your market should be your local area where referrals will bring you repeat and new business.

Keys to Success

Good word of mouth which you get by keeping your promises to deliver a quality product on time with no hidden costs.

Resources

Carlson Craft (top wholesaler of personalized papers, it's easy to become one of their dealers if you want to offer more types of stationery)
http://www.carlsoncraft.com/

Example of a similar business: FurSure (specializes in horses)
http://www.fursure.com/
Jocelyn Sandor
P.O. Box 546
Sherman, CT 06784

Example of business with charming but non-customized graphics:
Crane's Dog Notes http://www.crane.com/social/dognotes/
Also available at Papyrus chain stores and other fine stationers

81 Pet Taxi

General Concept

Busy, wealthy pet owners need someone to take Fido and Fluffy to the vet, the airport or play dates. You provide that service and transport one or many pets.

Profit Potential

May charge like other taxi drives on a per-mile basis plus fees for special services or offer a flat monthly fee for repeat customers for same destination. Limit geographical area being served or add a premium when you have to leave your local area.

Equipment Needed

Dependable car with substantial liability insurance. A van, station wagon or SUV works well. Crates and harnesses that attach to seat belts to keep pets safe and restrained while you drive. Cleanup products (like Nature's Miracle) for non-traffic accidents, and there will be many of them!

Project Startup Costs

Liability insurance for using a car for a business. Depending on your area, this may be in the thousands.

Pet restraint equipment (see above) at $200 or so. Have a cell phone for emergencies.

Getting Started

Get your business license, a chauffeur's driver's license and start handing out flyers or brochures at veterinarian offices, pet stores and condominium/apartment offices.

Be sure all marketing materials state which geographical areas you service (by zip code or name) and include a price schedule. This pre-screens clients and doesn't annoy those who don't want to be bothered having to call to get prices.

Pitfalls to Avoid

Develop a fee schedule for extra services. Clients may ask you to feed Fluffy or walk Fido before your trip. Be prepared to charge for these services. Time really is money.

Competition

Check your local phonebook. You shouldn't have too much competition yet.

Growth Potential & Expansion

Develop a relationship with local doggy or cat day care centers/boarding facilities to pick up their "clients" each day. Outfit a retired school bus or van to handle multiple fares.

Keys to Success

Patience, a love of animals and excellent driving record.

If possible, always bring one of the pet's favorite toys on the trip. Ask the client if the pet travels well and what to do if the pet gets car sick. Always have written permission before giving any food/beverage/medicine to a pet.

Resources

Sample website:
Canine Cab
http://www.caninecab.com

82 Publish Horse Friendly Guide

General Concept

You love your horse, you love travel (or have to travel); why not combine both interests by writing a guidebook about places that accommodate both you and your horse.

Profit Potential

Similar guidebooks for dogs and cats usually sell for $19.95.

Equipment Needed

You need a computer, preferably a laptop, with Internet connection and word processing software.

Getting Started

Select a geographical area to cover. It could be the entire U.S. or Canada or the East Coast. Whatever region you know or want to research. A narrower focus will be easier to market than a larger one and also will have less competition.

On the other hand, there should be enough horse owners and horse-friendly accommodations there to create a market for your product. Horse-Friendly Restaurants of Manhattan is unlikely to have much of a market.

Collect data for each entry: name, address, phone, email address, website, description of accommodations, prices, description of yard or stable and the nearby trails including steepness and difficulty. Plan on half-a-page for each entry.

101 Home based Businesses for Pet Lovers

Sources for listings are riding clubs, horse trainers, and horse shows. You'll spend a good deal of time on the Internet and be sure to include dude ranches.

This is a natural for self-publishing. Target horse-related businesses rather than bookstores as places to sell your book. See if the businesses will accept them on consignment.

Pitfalls to Avoid

Triple check all your facts and provide a way for readers to send you an email if an entry goes out of business or a website URL changes.

Growth Potential & Expansion

Sell advertising in your guidebook. Stores that sell horse-related supplies such as saddles and feed, or stables and riding academies, are potential advertisers.

Create a website for your book and sell it at amazon.com.

One woman has a successful subscription website called `http://www.d` for travelers who never leave home without Fido. She also has a print newsletter and sells products with her logo on them.

Another website (see Resources) provides a booking service for pet-friendly places and presumably gets a commission for each booking.

Competition

There are many guidebooks for dog and cat owners, but few that deal with horses. If you update your guidebook every 18-months of so, this could be a continuing way to earn money.

Keys to Success

Your creativity and marketing make you succeed or fail.

Resources

The Self-Publishing Manual:
How to Write, Print and Sell Your Own Book
(14th edition) by Dan Poynter
(Para Publishing, 2003, 432-pages)
Buy at www.amazon.com for $13.97

Example: Traveling With Horses
http://www.travelingwithhorses.com/

PET FRIENDLY Canada accommodations directory
http://petfriendly.ca/property/144.html
Accommodations as well as information on traveling with pets
http://www.destinationpets.com/Resource/Travel.htm

For networking:
Horse Hotel Club which is a Yahoo! group, register
at Yahoo! to participate.

83 PUBLISH LOCAL PET NEWSPAPER

General Concept

You publish a free monthly newspaper about pets in a targeted upscale, geographical area. For instance, The Beverly Hills (CA) Pet Journal. This publication is distributed in waiting rooms (veterinarians, groomers, etc) where pet owners congregate.

Profit Potential

Create a template of large, medium and small square blocks for ads. Sell each square anywhere from $22-$34 per issue for small to $250 for a front-page large square. Give discounts for long-term advertising.

Equipment Needed

Desktop publishing software, computer, scanner, printer and digital camera. Have copies run off at a local print shop or Office Depot. Don't overproduce. Sell the ads to determine how many pages you will publish that month. You don't need to do 20-pages to make money; you need to sell 20 adds.

Project Startup Costs

Depending how much equipment you already own, can be thousands to $100 for copying.

Getting Started

Decide on the paper (quality and size—newspaper style may be cheapest) and number of pages (4 to start if newspaper). Get estimate on how much it will cost to print and duplicate. Then add 10% and you have a rough estimate on the cost to publish.

Set up blank spaces on your page for ads to cover the costs of publication and whatever profit you want.

Take your template to all the pet-related businesses in your target area and see if you can sell enough ads to make it worthwhile to publish. Suggest they use the ad space for coupons for their businesses.

Pitfalls to Avoid

Don't try to do too much. Target your market and advertising base. Don't get hung up on editorial content. People are always interested in housebreaking tips.

Spend your time selling ads.

Growth Potential & Expansion

Add upscale geographical areas of about 25,000 as you able to deal with them. This is a tough business to run alone but can be done by two people.

Add classified section and get local professionals (vets, groomers, etc) to contribute columns in exchange for publicizing their business. Let people pay to add photos of their pets.

Competition

Don't attempt this if there's a competitor. The advertising base won't be there to support two publications.

Keys to Success

Sell ads!

101 Home based Businesses for Pet Lovers

Resources

Newsletter & Electronic Publishers Association
http://www.newsletters.org/
1501 Wilson Blvd., Suite 509
Arlington, VA 22209
Phone: 703.527.2333
E-mail: nepa@newsletters.org

Starting & Running a Successful Newsletter or Magazine
by Cheryl Woodard.
(Nolo Press, 3rd edition, 2002, 384-pages)
Available at www.amazon.com for $20.99

84 Puzzle Maker

General Concept

You create crossword puzzles or jigsaw puzzles based on a type of pet or customized for a particular pet. This business depends on having the right software to do the job. You can offer virtual (computer-based) puzzles or real puzzles.

Profit Potential

One company offering custom (your pet's photo) wooden jigsaws sells them for $65 for a 250-piece puzzle to $225 for a 1,000-piece puzzle. Non-customized puzzles unusually sell $10 to $60.

One website offering custom crossword puzzles sells 20 puzzles for $20. Another sells crossword puzzles customized for content AND shape for $100. You can create the crossword puzzle about a type of pet (e.g., cats) or from a list of words provided by the client (charge more for this).

Equipment Needed

You need a computer with Internet connection. Have plenty of memory for the graphics programs you'll need. Include photo-enhancing software such as Adobe Photoshop (about $600) or Microsoft Picture It (about $60). Include a color inkjet printer. If you do wooden or cardboard jigsaw puzzles, in addition to software, the fastest and easier way to do it is with a jigsaw puzzle press, which weighs about 500 pounds and costs around $9,000. (see http://www.serranorey.com/menu_other_products/jigsaw for an example)

101 Home based Businesses for Pet Lovers

You may want to do the marketing but use a commercial service (see Resources) for the actual manufacturing.

If you're handy and talented, you can make them by hand with a scroll saw but this is so time-consuming you may not be able to sell enough puzzles at a high-enough price to make it worthwhile. This, however, can be a satisfying hobby that may cover your expenses with a small profit. Baltic and Finnish birch are the preferred woods.

Getting Started

Develop your own puzzles and then create a website to display them.

Don't overlook the offline market for this. Many dog, cat and horse lovers are not computer literate but love to work crossword puzzles or cardboard jigsaw puzzles from a photo of their pet. Try small classified ads in free newspapers or your Sunday newspaper. If you develop a good product with a growing local market, try small classifieds in magazines devoted to your type of pet.

Distribute flyers to local pet stores, veterinarian offices, animal breeders, feed stores, and animal shows. Include a photo of the type of puzzle you're offering.

Pitfalls to Avoid

Do not violate any copyrights in the photos or graphics you use for the jigsaw puzzle. If customers provide you with the photos, include a statement on your order form that the customer is guaranteeing that they are the copyright holder.

Growth Potential & Expansion

Expand your computer-based puzzles with slide puzzles (one position in a frame is empty and the puzzle is solved by sliding pieces) or add more Flash or Shockwave puzzles.

Expand your offline business with greeting cards, calendars or posters. You can mix and match, for example, by adding a custom crossword or jigsaw puzzle to a greeting card.

Consider selling used puzzles, similar to used books. You buy other's puzzles and re-sell them. Many people love to do jigsaw puzzles but can't afford to buy as many new ones as they'd like.

Competition

There are many custom puzzle makers but almost none specialize in pets.

Keys to Success

Your creativity and marketing make you succeed or fail.

101 Home based Businesses for Pet Lovers

Resources

Software to create crossword puzzles
Crossword Weaver (top of the line about $40)
http://www.crosswordweaver.com/

Software to create virtual puzzles for your computer:
Jigsaw Power (about $50)
http://www.centronsoftware.com/

Example of websites selling custom wooden jigsaws:
Createajigsaw.com
http://www.createajigsaw.com/products.asp
J. C. Ayer & Co.
http://www.ayerpuzzles.com/faq.html

Puzzled Pets
(handmade puzzles of many types of pets about $30 each)
http://www.puzzledpets.com/

85 Raise Alpacas

General Concept

If you live in a rural area and have sufficient land and start-up capital, raising alpacas can be fun. They are generally good-natured animals. Best of all, this business doesn't involve killing the animal. You're breeding alpacas or shearing them.

Profit Potential

Alpaca profits lie in breeding. Alpacas meat is not desired in any country and the animals themselves are not otherwise work or pack animals. Investors buy a pregnant female and then sell her baby to industry newcomers seeking the romance of raising alpacas in a rural setting.

Neither the United States nor Canada has a large mill that commercially processes alpaca fiber from hair to sweater. That leaves domestic demand for fleece to cottage industries that typically pay about $2-4 an ounce for fleece, depending on fiber thickness. A typical alpaca produces between four to seven pounds a year.

Some alpaca farmers work around this by spinning their own fibers, knitting the garments and marketing the apparel on the Internet.

Equipment Needed

Alpacas do not require the same amount of land as most livestock. The rule of thumb is five-acres for 20 alpacas. The downside is that the animal itself is expensive, ranging from $7,500 to $40,000 depending on the gender.

The current world record price is $265,000 for an exceptional stud! Plan on $15,000 for equipment and increase that if you have to buy a pick-up truck.

You'll need shovel, water buckets, wheelbarrow, lead ropes, harnesses and toenail clippers.

Alpacas eat grass or hay so if your land isn't providing sufficient supplies, you'll need to buy feed. A special alpaca feed containing vitamins, minerals and protein pellets runs about $300 per year per animal.

Getting Started

If you don't already have it, get some experience working with alpacas or other type of livestock. Join the Alpaca Owners and Breeders Association, Inc. and get their informational CD/DVD. Then attend some alpaca auction sales/shows and see if you still want to get into the business.

Pitfalls to Avoid

The Alpaca Registry, Inc. (ARI) offers protection to alpaca owners because the registry has been closed since 1998 to any newly imported animals. It is very important for investors of alpacas to purchase only ARI registered alpacas. You will not be able to register alpacas unless both of their parents are currently registered with ARI. The ARI also will not recognize any alpaca unless it was produced naturally (i.e., no artificial insemination).

The ARI is intended to prevent the investment losses experienced by ostrich farmers several years ago. That industry saw breeding stock go from $70,000 a pair to $2,500 in a few years when the popularity of ostrich breeding collapsed. The ARI also lists blood type and DNA data to ensure breeding claims are accurate.

Alpacas are social animals. Do not expect to breed by paying a stud fee and trying to keep just one female alpaca. Also make sure you have insurance. Alpacas are more delicate than cattle and can easily harm themselves.

Growth Potential & Expansion

Learn to shear the alpacas—even if you just want to breed them. This is a skill that takes time to learn and is in demand. You can always make extra money if you know how to do this, and save a ton of money if you decide to market your own alpaca line of garments.

Competition

With fewer than 5,000 alpacas in the U.S., the supply is not saturated, but the problem is deciding where your market is—breeding, garments, or something else.

You may have trouble finding a vet who knows the alpaca anatomy. That's another reason to join the Alpaca Association and network with our breeders.

Keys to Success

Patience. It takes 11-months from gestation to birth of an alpaca. Then knowing what your market is and publicizing your product.

Resources

Alpaca Registry
http://www.alpacaregistry.net/
P.O. Box 87
Kalispell, MT 59903
Phone: 406.755.3158

Alpaca Owners and Breeders Association, Inc.
http://www.alpacainfo.com/
P.O. Box 1992
Estes Park, CO 80517-1992

86 Raise Birds

General Concept

You can take one of two paths. One is to raise pet birds for retail or wholesale.

The second path, if you live in a rural area with enough land, is to raise poultry for sale to wholesalers or raise game for sale for hunting or food consumption. A sideline is to sell eggs as there's a market for pheasant and quail eggs not to mention chicken eggs.

Profit Potential

Pet birds, depending on the species, sell for $40 to $75. You need to think of the first year as an investment while you buy the breeder birds, equip your home and breed the birds.

Don't try to undercut your local pet store, however, as you're unlikely to win that battle over the long haul, and there will always be people who prefer to go to a storefront pet store. A better strategy is to try to wholesale to pet stores.

A typical home-breeder averages two to three clutches or approximately 7 birds a year. Poultry and waterfowl can sell for $1 to $25 per bird depending on species.

Equipment Needed

Your largest initial outlay will be the purchase of the breeding birds. You need pairs (male and female). Plan on $50 to $100 each for pet birds. You need a brooder, weaning cages, formula, thermometers-for formula, and utensils to hand feed with and a few toys. This will be around $500 for all. Feed and vitamins will run approximately $40 to $50 a year per bird.

Visit your local feed store for supplies and recommendations on where to buy other equipment.

Getting Started

Canvass your local pet stores and see if they are interested in buying a particular breed of bird from you. If you can't find a cost effective way to market your birds, there is no point in breeding them.

Start with one of the heartier types of birds such as Cockatiels, Love Birds or Budgerigars rather than a canary or finch as the market is saturated with the latter two birds.

For pet bird breeding, you will need young, unrelated stock. It's better to buy males from one source and females from another. Another reason for buying young, untried birds is that established breeders who are continuing to breed will very seldom sell producing stock unless there are problems with the pairs.

Pitfalls to Avoid

The US Department of Agriculture has determined that birds will be regulated by the Animal Welfare Act. The USDA is in the process of establishing licensing requirements, minimum standards, and guidelines for inspections of facilities. Breeders, dealers, transporters, exhibitors, and carriers are all included at present, but how these terms will be defined is unclear. I strongly urge any bird breeder to join the The American Federation of Aviculture (see Resources) and remain current on this evolving piece of legislation.

Raise Birds

Most states also regulate the sale of animals. You must ensure you conform to all the laws in your state and locality.

Start with the purchase of high quality birds. You can't skimp here and expect to do well over the long haul. This will be your most expensive purchase.

You can't raise birds in rooms where other animals have been unless the rooms can be completely sterilized first. Birds are susceptible to bacterial and viral diseases that survive in wood, soil and other porous surfaces. One infection could wipe out your entire stock.

You will never make money with just one pair of birds. They don't understand that sometimes you may have to wait anywhere from 3 to 10 years for a pair of birds to figure out what they are doing.

Growth Potential & Expansion

Breed high quality birds whether for pets, food or game.

Competition

It depends on the species you select to breed and where you live. Areas with extreme temperatures (cold or hot) often lack many bird breeders.

Keys to Success

Learn to hand feed properly.

Find a veterinarian that specializes in birds. Not all vets understand birds or like to deal with them. You need to have a place to take a sick bird in an emergency.

Resources

The American Federation of Aviculture
(highly recommended for all)
http://www.afa.birds.org/
P.O. Box 7312
N. Kansas City, MO 64116
Phone: 816.421.2473

87 Raise Crickets

General Concept

You raise and sell crickets for other pet's food. Think of it as raising crops. Many exotic pets including frogs, lizards and turtles need to eat live food and crickets are one of the most popular. You can sell them to local pet stores and offer them for sale to the public in weekly free newspapers.

The Fish Odyssey pet store in Timonium, MD goes through 100,000 crickets a week!

Profit Potential

The normal life span of crickets is only a few weeks. Given that with their popularity as food for other pets and bait, there is a steady demand for live crickets.

Canvass local pet stores, bait shops and vets who handle exotic pets to see if a demand exists in your area.

Equipment Needed

$100 will cover all the supplies (except for crickets) that you need. Set up plastic storage containers (e.g., Rubbermaid or trash can), egg 'flats', heating pad from Wal-Mart, water fountain from a feed store (get the kind used for baby chicks), padding and aluminum mosquito screening. Keep them in the container with an open lid provided the container is high enough that they can't get out.

101 Home based Businesses for Pet Lovers

Getting Started

Start with a small order of breeder crickets (usually 250 is the minimum you can buy) for about $10 and see if you like doing this. Also order dry cricket feed from the same source for about $4 a pound. Crickets must be kept in a dry and warm climate (70s—80s) so make sure your home has sufficient heat if you live in a cold climate.

Females lay their eggs in a pan filled with mulch or peat moss. The eggs go into hatching flats (like egg cartons) where they incubate for close to two weeks.

Pitfalls to Avoid

They have a distinct odor and make a strange sound. They also tend to get loose. This is not the business for apartment dwellers!

You need a cricket sitter when you're going to be gone more than a day. Make sure the area you live in does not have any zoning or other regulations that prevent growing and having live insects.

Growth Potential & Expansion

In addition to live crickets, you can sell dried or frozen ones assuming you have the proper equipment. Beware though that both federal and state agricultural laws will apply if you ship crickets via mail.

Competition

Hobby breeders depress market values. Many people raise crickets for their own pets and once they see how easy it is, sell crickets at bottom-line prices. Survey pet stores and pet owners in your area before you make a decision to do this as a business.

Raise Crickets

Keys to Success

Feed the crickets a good quality cricket food. It's important to give them high nutrition so they will pass on their good nutrition when they're eaten. Using commercial food also helps prevent spread of diseases and infections.

Resources

Breeding and Raising the House Cricket
by Ian Hallett – only online at
http://www.anapsid.org/crickets.html

Southern Cricket Wholesaler Inc.
http://www.southerncricket.com/
P.O. Box 365
Nesbit, MS 38651
Phone: 800.545.6418

Example of someone doing this:
Bassetts Cricket Ranch
http://www.bcrcricket.com/
365 S. Mariposa
Visalia, CA 93292
Phone: 800.634.2445

88 Reminder Service

General Concept

You contract with pet related businesses to call their customers and remind them of appointments or to schedule appointments.

Profit Potential

You can expect to get $1 to $2 per customer call, depending on your area. This probably doesn't seem like much money but keep in mind that all you need is a telephone line and your operating costs are minimal.

Once you have some experience and some continuing volume customers, you may go to a monthly charge basis. For example, you might charge $35 per month for 70 calls with a surcharge of 25-cents per call beyond that.

Equipment Needed

You need a private telephone line and a reasonable toll and long-distance carrier. Have your customer reimburse you for any long distance calls.

You need a friendly telephone voice. Try taping yourself and make adjustments in your tone and diction as needed before you place actual calls to customers.

Getting Started

Call or visit local businesses and offer your service. Try local veterinarians and animal hospitals to get started and then move on to groomers and pet sitters.

Reminder Service

You can keep track of the calls you need to make by writing them on a calendar, creating index cards that are sorted by day and month or using software such as Microsoft Outlook where you enter the name and phone number to call and Outlook sends you a reminder on your computer. This is a nice way to do it.

Once you have enough customers to overtax your home telephone line, contact your local phone service to find out what options are available. This might include leasing a switchboard and cable installation if your customer base supports the increased costs.

Pitfalls to Avoid

Bill weekly or every other week. You don't want to let your charges grow so much that they look large to your customer. You also should offer direct electronic billing which your bank could help you set up.

Only do business during normal business hours—8 a.m. to 5 p.m. It's annoying for people to get phone calls at night, and you could too easily find that you're working all the time and missing out on family and recreation time. Do not use e-mail or fax for the reminder services unless your client has written consent forms from the people you'd be contacting. State and federal laws are restricting the use of unauthorized e-mail and fax. It doesn't matter if your customer has a relationship with the client you're faxing, your customer still needs written permission from the client. You could be held liable for violating the law if that written permission doesn't exist.

Growth Potential & Expansion

You could do this for other businesses such as accountants and bookkeepers, especially around tax time (January to April 15). Again, everyone else is competing for doctors and dentists so find other businesses that could use this service.

You also could provide a full telephone answering service for customers who don't have storefront offices and need someone to take their calls.

Another option is to team with a business that will pay you a commission for each sale made after you've made the appointment over the telephone. This works well for businesses like accountants and bookkeepers. Real estate offices do this but that market is very competitive.

Competition

Everyone else will be targeting doctors and dentists for this type of business so you may have your local animal industry to yourself.

Keys to Success

Pleasant phone voice and dependable service.

Reminder Service

Resources

Business by Phone, Inc.
operated by Art Sobczak
`http://businessbyphone.com/`
13254 Stevens St.
Omaha, NE 68137
Get his free report,
"42 Telesales Tips You Can Use Right Now to
Get More Business and Avoid Rejection" at his website.

Top Ten Telephone Basics (free web page)
`http://www.refresher.com/!shtelephone.html`

89 Sell Invisible Fencing

General Concept

You sell invisible fencing that works with a transmitter on Fido's collar to keep him safe at home. Many people have dogs but don't have fenced yards. Some communities have zoning or homeowner boards that forbid fences.

The invisible fence is an electric line buried a few inches down and around the perimeter of the yard. Whenever Fido tries to cross it, he gets an electric stimulation. It's just enough to remind him to stay put!

Profit Potential

Charge x-dollars per square yard. In my area, this is around $10 per square yard. Earnings of $40,000 a year are possible if you have enough dogs and unfenced yards in your area.

Equipment Needed

You'll need inventory and digging equipment. Depending on what you own, this could run you $10,000 to $15,000. You'll also need a vehicle that can haul the fencing and digging equipment. Look for something used.

Getting Started

Leave flyers at homes with dogs and without fences. Something like the following: "We install invisible fencing. Keep your dog safe at home and avoid disputes with your neighbors. Call xxx-xxxx for a free estimate."

Also leave flyers or business cards at veterinarian offices.

Sell Invisible Fencing

Pitfalls to Avoid
You need ability to dig and some electrical competence.

Growth Potential & Expansion
Contact manufacturers and buy the fencing wholesale.

Competition
Not many companies specialize in this but several do-it-yourself systems are sold through hardware stores.

Keys to Success
Do a good job and get referrals.

Resources

Manufacturers who use dealers:
Invisible Fence Inc.
http://www.ifco.com/

DogWatch Inc.
http://www.dogwatch.com/

90 Sell Mobile Bird Cages

General Concept

You design and build a portable, travel cage suitable for birds. Most of the products out there are just cat or dog cages being marketed as bird cages.

Profit Potential

Prices vary by the size of the bird. Typical cockatoo cage is about $60, while a macaw cage is $90 to $130.

Equipment Needed

Decide on materials you want to use - steel, netting, PVC pipe, Plexiglas - the sky's the limit. But be sure to include wooden perches/play bars, and a feeding pan that slides out so people don't have to put their hand in the cage to feed the bird.

Getting Started

Try to get a local pet store to carry your product. Sell them at local flea markets. Create unusual and exotic designs and covers to distinguish yourself from the mass market. If they seem popular, advertise in the *Companion Parrott Quarterly* (see Resources).

Pitfalls to Avoid

Don't overextend yourself. Sell slowly and ensure you have a good design that bird owners like.

Sell Mobile Bird Cages

Growth Potential & Expansion

Keep expanding your line so that any bird has a size appropriate cage. If your designs are popular, sell the plans separately in the do-it-yourself market.

Competition

Check pet stores and bird magazines to see what the competition is selling.

Keys to Success

Design for a bird. Have bird-specific bar spacing, bird-safe finishes and the ability to adjust bars to suit an Amazon or a cockatoo.

Require no assembly and make them able to be folded up when not in use.

Resources

Companion Parrot Quarterly
P.O. Box 2428
Alameda, CA 94501-0254
Phone: 510.523.5303

For ideas, try these websites:
http://bird-cage-plans.bravepages.com
http://www.geocities.com/tuckergold/birdcage.html

How to Build Everything You Need for Your Birds, from Aviaries...to Nestboxes by Dominic LaRosa available at http://www.amazon.com/ for $15

91 Set Up Koi Ponds

General Concept

In this business, you can do everything yourself or just arrange everything yourself. Provide the design for the pond, hire contractors to install it and then stock the pond with koi. If that seems like too much work, limit your business to providing regular maintenance of koi ponds, similar to swimming pool maintenance outfits.

As koi can live 30 to 100 years, maintenance can be a very nice business! Thanks to its enduring popularity with Baby Boomers, koi ponds continue to be one the most frequent additions to upscale homes.

Profit Potential

Typical koi sell anywhere from $10 to $125 each. High quality show or breeder koi can cost more than $25,000 while the current record is $850,000 for one koi. Your services will vary by your locality. Contractors building a koi pond will get more than a weekly maintenance service, but over the long haul, a regular maintenance service will provide the better income.

A typical koi backyard pond can have 5,000 to 20,000 gallons of water with waterfalls, spillways, filters, oxygenators, aerators, landscape and backup generators. Then add the fish. Best of all, you can broker or sell all of it!

Equipment Needed

Breeding pair(s) of koi if you do it yourself or a wholesale source if you want to buy and re-sell them. As koi can weigh 25 to

Set Up Koi Ponds

30 pounds, commercial koi food including pellets of whitefish meal, wheat-germ meal, spirulina, vitamins, and minerals can get expensive.

A koi pond must have a filter system and pump operating 24-hours a day. At a minimum all pond water volume must be pumped through the filter system every two hours. The pond should be at least 3 1/2 feet deep. The rule of thumb is one fish for each 100 gallons of water.

Getting Started

There are about 25 koi shows across the U.S. each year. Attend as many as you can to learn about these popular fish. Then join the nearest koi club (there's 100+) and participate in their annual pond tours. (See Resources)

Leave your flyers at home improvement, garden stores and nurseries. The same kind of people who like gardens, like ponds.

Place classified ads in Sunday newspapers and free-classified ad papers.

Pitfalls to Avoid

Koi are subject to parasites and bacteria infections. You must keep the water quality high and have a filter system free of sharp or abrasive objects.

Don't buy or sell koi at shows. The poor chemistry of the water, tank environment and the stress on the fish from traveling and handling may cause the koi's health to deteriorate and result in high mortality rates.

After you buy a new koi, quarantine it prior to adding it to an existing pond. Koi are very susceptible to parasites, and you don't want to infect an entire community.

If you are a contractor, you must have all city, state licenses and sufficient insurance. It may be more economical to refer clients to contractors who pay you a referral fee.

Growth Potential & Expansion

Team up with landscape architects to create a total backyard environment and with contractors who build koi ponds.

Competition

Depends on the area of the country; however, koi like cold water so they're not confined to Southern states. There are several do-it-yourself koi pond kits, but your market should be older, upscale people who don't have the time or talent to do this kind of work.

Keys to Success

Breed or sell only healthy fish which also requires maintaining a high quality of water.

Do offer short guarantees (48-hours is typical) but insist customers return to you dead or diseased koi.

Set Up Koi Ponds

Resources

Associated Koi Clubs of America
for a list of clubs and shows
http://www.akca.org/

Koi Carp monthly magazine
http://www.koi-carp.com/home/news.asp
Freestyle Publications Ltd
Koi Carp Subscriptions
Alexander House, Ling Road, Tower Park,
Poole, Dorset BH12 4NZ.
England

92 Show Exotic Pets

General Concept

If you already keep some pets beyond the standard dog and cat, you may have a potential business putting on shows for children and other animal lovers. By exotic pets, we mean pets such as pythons, turtles, chameleons, rabbits and salamanders.

Profit Potential

Charge per event, typically $50 to $200 depending on how many animals you have to transport and how long the event lasts. You really need 10-12 pets to make it a worthwhile show.

Equipment Needed

Other than dependable transportation, you need to own the pets or have access to them. Your cheapest and best source of marketing will be to paint your vehicle with your business name and phone number. If you have a van, paint it all over with as much information as possible. If you own or keep the pets, you need premium quality feed and regular veterinary exams to ensure the animals are healthy and do not pass any viral or bacterial infections to your audience (and vice versus).

Getting Started

Get licensed and insured. Make sure you have liability insurance; look at umbrella policies. A pet could get loose and cause some damage. Also if you have an expensive, rare pet you may want business insurance to cover the loss if the pet should die suddenly or be injured.

Show Exotic Pets

Children's birthday parties are an ideal place to start. What elementary school boy wouldn't love to have a python slither down his arm or be able to stroke a lizard? Just ensure you select non-poisonous animals and never let a child alone with the animal.

Distribute your flyers to Parent-Teacher groups and schools. Leave flyers at businesses frequented by elementary school children and their parents. Contact school principals and offer your services.

Market your business as an animal education and entertainment experience and provide educational information as part of the demonstration. Don't neglect telling funny stories that kids will enjoy.

If you enjoy this and the audience seems to like you expand to senior centers.

Once you have your act down, create marketing materials and run a small classified ad in the local newspaper offering your party services. If your area has professional party planners, send them your flyer or business card.

Pitfalls to Avoid

The pets may be exotic in that everyone doesn't have one but they should always be safe ones. This is a business to start only if you already have or had such types of pets and understand them.

Laws vary by location. Check with a local lawyer to ensure you don't need special licensing to have reptiles or other exotic pets. Not all types of pets are permitted in every state or city.

Growth Potential & Expansion

If you live in an area with professional event planners, try to team with one to create jungle-themed parties using your exotic pets.

You can increase your income by offering a full party package rather than just getting paid to be an entertainer. If you can offer a full "Crocodile Hunter" themed birthday party, you can charge a great deal more than $200 for a performance.

Competition

Very little competition exists outside of major metropolitan areas.

Keys to Success

If you have a gift for entertaining, love handling these types of pets and are dependable, this is a business you can enjoy running for many years.

Resources

For an example of such a business:
Pet-Shows-on-Wheels
http://www.expage.com/page/lagamorphs

93 Start Niche Magazine

General Concept

You find a pet population that is too small for the general magazines but with enough devotees to support a magazine dedicated to the pet. The model for this business is *Modern Ferret* magazine with 23,000 circulation. A couple started it in 1994 with $10,000 because they couldn't get relevant ferret-care information from other mainstream pet publications.

Profit Potential

The sky's the limit. Note that if you want to accept commercial advertising (as opposed to classified ads), advertisers may insist on slick magazine-type paper so photographs reproduce well rather than newsprint or regular white paper.

Equipment Needed

You need a computer with word publishing software. I like Microsoft Publisher as it is extremely user friendly and comes with templates. If you want to include photographs, you'll need a digital camera.

Getting Started

Visit the Magazine Publisher's website for articles. (See Resources.)

Even if you don't want advertising from commercial companies, you may want to offer classified ads for subscribers. Decide what type of paper you want to use and lay out a sample issue.

As this publication is national rather than local, mail announcements of your new publication to manufacturers of products that serve your pet if you're going to accept advertising. Include a rate card for ads. You can get names of manufactures off the products you use or visit the it Thomas Register at your local library.

Send out press releases to general pet magazines, the business magazines (*Pet Age* and *Pet Business*) for pet stores and any hobby groups you can locate. Also announce your new publication on appropriate discussion boards (search Google Groups if you don't know any).

You can try small classified ads in publications that have a larger audience that would include your niche target group.

Pitfalls to Avoid

This is a time commitment you must be willing to undertake. Also think about how you want to end your enterprise when you're tired of meeting monthly deadlines. You may want to start with just three-month subscriptions so you can kill the publication if it doesn't take off the way you think it will (or should).

Take it small and slow. Don't kill yourself trying to do too much the first month. You can grow your publication over the months.

Use a template and don't waste time on format. Content makes these publications grow. Don't give away free sample issues. If you have selected the right topic, people will be paying a single copy price (12 divided by annual subscription price) to sample the product.

Start Niche Magazine

Growth Potential & Expansion

Unlimited potential with back-end products. The couple who started *Modern Ferret* now sell books, ferret toys, food, beds, calendars, T-shirts, sweatshirts, mugs, mouse pads, license plate frames and posters among other things! Where else would you go for products designed for ferrets?

Competition

Don't get into this if there's any competition.

Keys to Success

Pick a rare pet with no competing publications. You will not succeed trying to compete against *Dog Fancy* or *Cat Fancy*, even if you think you have the superior product.

101 Home based Businesses for Pet Lovers

Resources

Modern Ferret (for inspiration)
http://www.modernferret.com/
P.O. Box 1007
Smithtown, NY 11787
$27.95 for a year's subscription

Starting and Running a Successful Newsletter or Magazine
by Cheryl Woodard
(Nolo Press, 384 pages, 2002)
$20.99 at www.amazon.com

Magazine Publishers of America (trade association)
http://www.magazine.org/
919 Third Avenue
New York, NY 10022
Phone: 212.872.3700
E-mail: infocenter@magazine.org

94 Stock Photos and Drawings

General Concept

You use your creative talents to develop stock photos of animals or original line drawings that can be licensed for use offline and online.

It can be difficult to find quality royalty-free photos of pets that people can use in newsletters, websites and advertising. You can sell your products as clip art for one-time fees.

Profit Potential

One website sells a CD-ROM containing original drawings of all dog breeds for $30 with additional fees $100+ for custom work. Another website sells a CD-ROM of 99 Corel dog photos for $99 plus shipping.

Equipment Needed

You need a camera or supplies for the type of artwork you will create. You need a source of pets for models, and you should ensure the models conform to any breed standards that apply to the pet.

Getting Started

Create your work and send out flyers to pet businesses especially websites and publishers who need this type of product.

Get listed with the websites and publications that offer stock photography or other artwork (see Resources).

Create CD-ROMs and DVDs of your products and sell them everywhere including on eBay. Run small classified ads in pet publications targeted to businesses. Many publishers need this type of product but have no idea where to find it.

Pitfalls to Avoid

Never use a photograph or drawing if you don't know the source and don't have a release.

Growth Potential & Expansion

You can offer custom services of your artwork and you can act as an agent for other photographers or artists.

Competition

There are a limited number of suppliers of this type of product. Corel:
`http://www.corel.com/servlet/Satellite?pagename=Corel/Home`
has some of the best products and is the most well known.

Keys to Success

The reason people buy your product rather than getting a $5 CD-ROM via eBay is to get a product that is legal to use. Businesses do not want to be sued or fined for copyright infringements, and there is no way to know the source and legality of using much of the art work purchased over eBay. You must provide original works or you must have release forms from any pet owner whose photograph you take. Visit `http://www.nolo.com` for samples of release forms.

People also do not want a continuing license fee for the use of the products. You should establish a one-time fee for use with no further payments or restrictions other than withholding the right of the buyer to re-sell or distribute your art or photographs

Stock Photos and Drawings

as stock photography or clipart. Take a look at Corel and other clipart manufacturers license agreements for examples of applicable language.

Resources

Examples of original drawings:
Ahead, All Breed Clipart
http://www.aheadgraphics.com/ahead5.htm
E-mail: ahead@aheadgraphics.com
For information on starting and running this business:
Rohn Engh's PhotoSource International
(a must visit if you're doing photography)
http://www.photosource.com/index.php
Pine Lake Farm
1910 35th Road
Osceola, WI 54020-5602
Sell and Re-Sell Your Photos
by Rohn and Ron Engh (a classic)
(Writers Digest Books, 5th edition, 2003, 374-pages)
available at www.amazon.com for $13.99

Example of joint website that sells stock photographs of cats:
Aigrette Stockpix.com
http://stockpix.com/stock/animals/domesticanimals/cats/index.htm
93559 Easy Creek Ln.
Coos Bay, OR 97420

95 SUMMER CAMP FOR DOGS

General Concept

If you live in a tourist area or want a way to afford to spend the summer in a tourist area, operate a summertime only camp for dogs. Tourists who want to travel with Fido but spend their days on the golf courses in Hilton Head won't need to worry about Fido because he will be swimming, canoeing and socializing at your summer camp.

This can be a nice business for someone who wants to spend the summer on say, the Oregon coast but couldn't afford to do it just as a tourist. There are plenty of dog owners who want to spend the summer at the same places you do. Happily, enough of them can afford to pay for your service.

Profit Potential

Offer prices for the day, weekend and week. One summer camp in Canada charges $150 for weekends. This is a luxury item for pet owners who think of Fido as their child so price accordingly. Canvass local dog day-care centers to see what they charge and at least double that if you're keeping the dog all night.

Have dog owners pay a non-refundable reservation fee to hold a spot but don't accept the dog and get final payment until you've interviewed both parties.

Equipment Needed

You need an area that allows multiple dogs and that has sufficient natural features or man made ones to be a recreational area for dogs. Ensure that you meet all zoning and public health

Summer Camp for Dogs

requirements. You don't need a year-round area. You can lease part of a field or agricultural area for the summer.

You don't need to spend much money on buildings, as the dogs won't care as long as they have a safe and habitable facility to take naps and to get away from bad weather. Temporary buildings and even large recreational vehicles will do.

You will need liability insurance. Check with major carriers to see if you can get a short-term umbrella coverage for the period the summer camp operates.

Getting Started

Find your spot and set up a schedule for the busy camper.

Send out flyers to news media, pet clubs, pet businesses, local Chamber of Commerce and tourism offices.

Pitfalls to Avoid

Insist on evidence of vaccinations for each dog.

Don't accept a camper until you've personally interviewed the dog and feel confident that he can participate in a group setting. Not all dogs can. It's a good idea to have a friendly, well-trained dog with you when you interview the dogs to see how they react to one another.

Growth Potential & Expansion

You add agility training if you are trained in this.

Many dog camps also accept the dog owners although this requires more area, stable infrastructure and increases the regulations and liability applicable to your camp.

Competition

This is a young industry with minimal competition.

Keys to Success

You need to be available 24/7 or have family or staff to help you so you can take a break when you need to. As much as you may love dogs, playing with them and listening to barking all day will eventually get on your nerves. Schedule regular break times to refresh your temperament.

Resources

For examples:
Dog Days of Wisconsin LLC
http://www.dogcamp.com/
235 S Greenfield Ave
Waukesha, WI 53186
E-mail: summercamp@dogcamp.com

Camp Winnaribbun at Lake Tahoe, NV
http://www.campw.com/
P.O. Box 50300
Reno, NV 89513
E-mail: info@campw.com

96 Tour Operator

General Concept

If you live in a popular tourist area, you can make extra money by operating pet friendly tours for people who insist on traveling with Fido and Fluffy. You identify attractions and areas that allow pets and provide transportation along with an entertaining spiel.

In some cases, it may just be the transportation and spiel that you provide. Commercial tour company buses generally allow only companion animals; e.g., seeing-eye dogs. You can drive Fido and his owners around while they all look at the local tourist traps without getting out (save bathroom breaks!).

You can run this business part-time, on weekends or evenings.

Profit Potential

This is unlikely to be a full-time business but $20 to $50 per person, depending on length of the tour, can supplement your income and be fun to do at the same time. Figure your costs (mainly transportation and insurance) and add 40% or so to develop your per-person charge.

Equipment Needed

How will you get your tour clients to the attractions? You may need to lease a tour bus or van and get a commercial or chauffeur's driver license from your state if you plan on doing the driving. Alternately, you may rent a bus and driver from local bus company as the need arises. In either case, make sure you have sufficient insurance coverage for accidents and adhere to your state's laws regarding commercial transportation of people. Your vehicle, whether leased, owned or rented, will need to be accessible to the handicapped.

Always have emergency pet equipment, such as leashes and collars, and products including some type of pooper scooper to clean up the inevitable accidents.

Getting Started

Send out flyers or brochures to all the pet friendly attractions in your area. Leave flyers at pet stores, pet businesses and all the hotels and inns that allow pets.

Get listed in all the pet friendly websites and publications you can locate through Google and pet publications.

Growth Potential & Expansion

You can develop a website or publication (newsletter, book, etc) and charge for listing other pet friendly attractions.

You can establish packages for tourists with coupons for pet friendly attractions or hotels and charge businesses to include their coupons, similar to Money Mailer and other coupon packages that come in the mail. Remember that most health codes don't allow pets in restaurants (except for seeing-eye dogs, etc) so don't count on many restaurants participating.

You also can contract with pet service businesses; e.g., groomers, to hand out coupons for their services to your clients. You get a referral fee each time a customer uses the pet business and turns in the coupon.

Competition

There's unlikely to be much competition among pet-friendly tours.

Tour Operator

What is highly competitive and difficult to run is a home-based travel agency. Many try the latter but few make money at it. Not recommended unless you're already a travel agent and just want to operate from home.

Keys to Success

You must be knowledgeable about locations and experiences that will appeal to tourists and their pets and have the outgoing, upbeat personality a tour guide requires.

Pitfalls to Avoid

If you lease a tour bus or van, get a non-refundable deposit (or payment in full) from people when they sign up for the tour. You can let customers use their deposit for another time if they're unable to take a planned tour, but you won't stay in business long if you don't have sufficient cash flow to cover your transportation costs.

If you team with a travel agency, make it a local one and never pay an agency in order to become a commission salesperson for them.

Resources

The National Tour Association (expensive memberships)
http://www.ntaonline.com/
546 East Main Street
Lexington, KY 40508
E-mail to questions@ntastaff.com

How to Start a Specialty Travel & Tour Business:
Your Step-by-Step Guide to Success
by Rob Adams (Entrepreneur Media Inc., 2003, 180-pages) available at www.amazon.com for $10.47

97 Upscale Pet Products

General Concept

You make very expensive items for pampered pets. The model for this type of business is the Pet Feather, a feather boa for the dog who has everything else. Both *Pet Product News* and *Entrepreneur* magazines rated this product as one of the best for 2002. With product names such as Muttini Toy Collection in colors such as Little Blue Boa Bikini Bitch from High Maintenance Bitch (the name of the company, not a comment), you understand these are very upscale items. The company recently added a boa line for cats.

Profit Potential

The sky's the limit. High Maintenance Bitch company expects to sell $1M worth of dog and cat boas this year. The boa retails for around $30.

Equipment Needed

You can make products yourself and probably need to until you perfect a design. Then find a manufacturer through your library's copy of the it Thomas Register who can manufacture in bulk.

Getting Started

Read the publications targeted to pet businesses. These are *Pet Age* and *Pet Business*. Join the American Pet Products Manufacturers Association. Besides networking and learning

Upscale Pet Products

about the trade shows, this organization has helpful information on various laws affecting pet products.

Attend trade shows and see what types of products are popular and what the trends are. Don't be afraid to approach retail pet store buyers and ask them what kind of product their customers ask for and can't find.

Once you have a prototype, take your product to your local pet stores and see if they want to carry it. Try selling it at craft fairs and flea markets. You need customer feedback to tell if you have a winner and what you could do to improve the design.

Pitfalls to Avoid

Don't develop a product no one wants, and you can't market. Test samples before you invest money in large production runs. Develop a design and a prototype and then try to sell it on eBay, listed under several categories.

Growth Potential & Expansion

Attend pet product trade shows and contract with some independent salespeople to market your product across the country.

Competition

Find a way to distinguish your product from any comparable ones. You may be as fortunate as High Maintenance Bitch to have a product that's unique, but if not, you can use marketing and product name to distinguish yourself.

Note—unique products don't remain unique for very long, copycats are everywhere. Your reliable service to retailers will help ensure you remain in business while the copycats flock to copy other, newer products (forgive the mixed metaphors).

101 Home based Businesses for Pet Lovers

Keys to Success

Developing a product with the right appeal and then marketing it continuously.

Many pet stores do not like to do business with small, one or two product companies because they feel the businesses are not professional and reliable and can't handle shipping problems and returns. Talk to your local pet storeowner or manager about their pet peeves with small manufacturers and find ways to reassure the pet store personnel that you have these problems under control.

Have a plan to deal with emergencies and shipping problems. If you're a one woman or man business, who will handle problems while you're at trade shows? You may need to hire a fulfillment service or draft relatives/friends to help out. Have contingency plans in place for the most common types of emergencies such as lost shipments.

As you market continuously, compare prices on suppliers continuously. Take advantage of websites that compare prices and ensure you are paying the least possible price for the supplies you need and services such as shipping.

Resources

For an example of this type of product:
High Maintenance Bitch (pet boas)

American Pet Products Manufacturers Association, Inc.
(the trade organization)
http://www.appma.org
255 Glenville Road
Greenwich, CT 06831
Phone: 203.532.0000

98 Video or DVD Producer

General Concept

Would you buy a DVD with an hour's worth of moths flying around? Pretty boring, right? Unless you're a cat, and then it's a best seller. Really.
http://kittyshow.com/bugsdvdinfo.htm

This DVD has been mentioned in the Wall Street Journal and USA Today. Remember—these DVDs, CDs and videos are for pets, not people.

Profit Potential

Special interest DVDs or videos retail for $19.95 to $24.95. Sometimes more. Considering that DVD reproduction costs are around $2 each, you can see the profit potential if you pick a winning topic.

More than 100-million American homes have some type of pet. Cats and birds are the ideal market because they have a longer attention span than dogs.

Equipment Needed

None—rent everything. You can get the latest technology. See if you like production and if there's a market for your product(s) before you sink costs into expensive equipment. When you have sufficient cash flow from your sales, you can buy new equipment and get a tax deduction. Take a course on DVD or video production from a local community college. Alternately, hire someone to tape or film the product for you. There are tons of amateur or professional video makers for hire.

101 Home based Businesses for Pet Lovers

Getting Started

Pick a pet you know and like. Then record a program that would appeal to them, not you.

Do the editing in a rented-studio (large cities have places that rent by the hour) or hire someone to edit and add music for you.

Send your product to a commercial duplicator rather than doing it yourself. That will ensure your product will play on 99.9% of the computers or players out there and remove the problem of homemade labels jamming DVD players.

Get your product listed at http://www.amazon.com/. Read about the amazon.com Marketplace and Advantage programs and decide which one is right for you.

Don't forget to offer your product at http://www.ebay.com.

Pitfalls to Avoid

The biggest mistake you can make is buying equipment before you understand what you really need (which isn't as much as you'll want to buy).

Don't try to duplicate the media yourself. A paper label you create and stick on a DVD may harm the client's DVD player. Using a professional duplicator company ensures compatibility with almost every player sold.

Growth Potential & Expansion

Develop a customer list and add to the line. If you can sell a cat owner one DVD, you can sell him two or three more. Ask all customers to fill out a self-addressed, stamped postcard with their addresses or e-mail addresses for notices of special offers. Then notify them when you have a new product.

Video or DVD Producer

Sell other people's products as well. Create a website, mail order or eBay store and add more products for your type of pet.

Get an Universal Product Code (UPC). That's needed if you want amazon.com. bn.com, Wal-Mart or Costco to handle your products. It's expensive to get one so see if your DVD duplicator (e.g., `http://www.discmakers.com`) will provide it.

Competition

There are some 36-million cat owners in America and probably fewer than 10 production companies dedicated to making products for cats.

Keys to Success

The right product. Play your finished product for several pets in your target market and make sure they like it.

Market constantly. Send out press releases to 300 publications or websites. See if local pet stores will carry your product. Send a sample to magazines that specialize in your type of pet and ask for reviews.

Resources

For cats:
`http://www.cattv.com/VideosforCats.htm`

For dogs:
`http://www.speedvd.com/daycaretext.html`

For birds:
`http://www.parrottricktraining.com/`

99 Virtual Cemetery and Memorial Center

General Concept

You operate a website that allows pet owners to honor the memory of their deceased pets by erecting virtual tombs and memorials on the website. This business could be an adjunct to a real pet cemetery or a stand-alone business. Many people want to remember their pets in a more vital setting than a cemetery.

The virtual tomb basic package would be a photograph of the late pet and a few lines written by the mourners. For an additional fee, the mourners may add video or audio files of the late pet so that family and friends can always hear and see the pet in action.

Many pet owners love to write poems about their deceased pets. By placing them on your website, they are available to the mourner and the pet's other friends and extended family at all times. The pet owner does not have to worry about maintaining Internet service or website maintenance.

Profit Potential

Charge an annual fee to establish a memorial for the pet. The website example in Resources charges $30 a year for a basic listing. Charge an additional fee if you design the virtual tomb and write the obituary.

Virtual Cemetery and Memorial Center

Equipment Needed

Computer with Internet access and software to build a website and retouch photographs.

Getting Started

Create a website and place one or two memorials on your website. Use your own late pets or those of other family members.

You need to decide whether every visitor will be able to see all the memorials or if you want to create separate web pages with URLs known only to a customer (or password protected). Perhaps you want to offer both and charge an additional fee for web page security when desired.

This is an unusual business that may be attractive to news media. Send out press releases to your local news media as well as commercial publications that serve pet owners, e.g., *Cat Fancy* magazine, *Horse Illustrated* magazine or *Modern Ferret*. Develop a flyer and leave at pet businesses and veterinarians in your local area.

Pitfalls to Avoid

Your website must look dignified and be respectful of the deceased and their mourners. Avoid hyped marketing piteches.

Growth Potential & Expansion

You may offer virtual services for people who lost their pet in circumstances that did not allow full closure. For example, people temporarily living outside of the United States may only be able to have this type of memorial for their pet. You also might sell memorial supplies including religious ones.

Competition

There are virtual pet cemeteries on the Internet. You may want to specialize in a geographical area to make your website stand out.

Keys to Success

You must get high rankings in the Internet search engines. Make certain your website is optimized to rank well on Google, see `http://www.google.com/webmasters/` and the other major search engines.

Resources

For an example of a business doing this:
World Gardens `http://www.worldgardens.com/`
3761 Citation Way #511
Myrtle Beach, SC 29577

Virtual Pet Cemetery (specializes in California pets)
`http://www.pets.ca/petsites/index_cemetery.php`

Genealogy.com Virtual Cemetery (this is a huge website)
`http://www.genealogy.com/vcem_welcome.html`

100 WRITE A GUIDE FOR WOULD-BE BREEDERS

General Concept

You write *A Guide to Raising Rare Breed* (Dogs, Cats, Lizards, Snakes, whatever type of pet you know) *for Profit*. Many people who love animals would like to breed their favorite type of pet but lack the know-how to get started.

Profit Potential

You can try to sell your book to a publisher or self-publish. Depending on your sales and whether you have a publisher or not, your royalties on the retail sales price can net you anywhere from $1 a copy to $9 a copy.

With amazon.com and bn.com, however, there are great opportunities for self-publishers today. If you self-publish and sell just 500 copies, you still have the potential to make a four-figure profit, maybe more.

Equipment Needed

You need a computer with Internet access and a word processing program, preferably Microsoft Word. You can use a desktop publishing program such as PageMaker but that's not necessary.

Your knowledge and research are the major tools you need.

Getting Started

Your guide needs to be at least 100 pages and formatted along the lines of *Entrepreneur Magazine*'s Business Start Up Guides.

Get one from your library or buy one to see how they're formatted. You'll need to cover start up costs, recommended breeds, vet advice, sources for needed equipment, and marketing suggestions. This should not be targeted as a get-rich-quick book but rather as an intelligent discussion of the opportunities and pit falls of becoming your type of breeder.

Pitfalls to Avoid

Know what you're talking about. Do your homework and do select a pet you like and know yourself.

Research the laws relating to your pet. You don't want to write about raising an exotic pet that cannot legally be bred in captivity or sold across state lines. Many states have different laws and some, such as California, are complex and extensive in the area of breeding. You might want to pay a lawyer who specializes in animal laws for an hour of his/her time before you undertake your book.

Growth Potential & Expansion

If the book sells well, develop a newsletter or subscription website related to the book and start thinking about the next edition.

Don't forget to publish your book as an e-book and on CD-ROM. Both can be sold at www.amazon.com.

Competition

There are many general-themed breeding books (e.g., breed dogs or breed cats), but not many specialize in one breed and few specialize in the more exotic pets such as leopard geckoes, basilisks, or iguanas. Yet, there is a market for these types of pets.

Write a Guide for Would-Be Breeders

Keys to Success

Marketing your book will be the major effort. Send review copies to any magazine or newsletter that is related to your type of breed and offer a discounted price for people who order prior to publication.

Get your book carried by Quality Books distributors who service libraries across the country.

Read both or one of the books recommended in Resources for an explanation of how to do this.

Market to pet stores that carry your type of pet. Approach local stores and superstores. If there are breeding or fan clubs for your type of pet, send them a publicity release about your book. For local clubs, offer to give a presentation on your book.

Resources

Writer's Digest has numerous special magazines on getting started, writing nonfiction and getting published. Visit your local Barnes & Noble or Borders bookstore for copies. These two books are worth reading even if you want to sell your book to a publisher rather than self publish.

The Self-Publishing Manual:
How to Write, Print and Sell Your Own Book (14th edition)
by Dan Poynter
(Para Publishing, 2003, 432-pages)
Buy at www.amazon.com for $13.97

The Complete Guide to Self-Publishing
by Tom and Marilyn Ross.
(F&W Publications, 2002, 521-pages)
Buy at www.amazon.com for $13.99

An example of one breeder who wrote a guide for breeders:
Confessions of a Cat Breeder
http://www.confessionsofacatbreeder.com/intro.html

101 YELLOW PAGES DIRECTORY

General Concept

You don't have to use yellow pages but if you live in or near a large urban area, you can create a business directory with contact information including e-mail and URLs of pet related businesses in your area. This is a good idea if you live in Houston, TX and a poor one if you live in Black Duck, N.D.

Profit Potential

Display ads can sell for more in directories because they remain in a customer's home longer. See the explanation under *Getting Started* on how to price your ads and listings.

Equipment Needed

You need a computer with desktop publishing software such as Microsoft Publisher or the more expensive products such as QuarkXPress. You need dependable transportation for your sales calls and to distribute your product.

Getting Started

Create a draft cover and inside pages with placeholders for display ads and telephone listings. If you don't have any graphic arts talent, hire a college art student to create an attractive cover.

Price paper, printing and distribution. You can print it yourself if you have a large capacity laser printer or use one of the office supply stores to do the reproduction. You also can distribute the directories yourself or hire a local company or students to do it. If you intend to mail the product, price postage at different weights.

Based on your costs, add a fudge factor and your desired profit, then determine your price per page. Now layout a couple pages with different size ads and one just with four or five line listings. Assign a price to each size ad and listing. In other words, if a page should sell for $480 and you create six display ads of the same size on a page, then each ad should sell for $80.

Take your draft product around to pet related businesses and find out if enough will buy your product to make it worthwhile to have it printed in bulk. If there isn't a sufficient market for the product, refund any money you've gotten and try another business.

You can distribute the directories at libraries, pet stores and pet shows. Also get a listing from your local government of people who purchased dog and cat licenses and send post cards to those in affluent areas (look at zip codes) with information on how to order a directory.

Pitfalls to Avoid

Charge enough per ad and listing so you hire a distributor. You won't get advertisers if they don't believe you will be distributing the directories to enough potential customers.

Growth Potential & Expansion

You can expand to other nearby large areas and even offer a statewide directory if your state is small enough.

Most niche yellow pages are given free to customers and rely on advertising and listings to cover costs and profit. There

YELLOW PAGES DIRECTORY

is no reason, however, you couldn't charge a nominal amount especially if you intend to mail your directory.

Competition

It's unlikely there are any pet-related, hard copy yellow page directories in your area. More and more businesses are relying on Internet directories, but there is still a large market of people who rarely if ever use a computer and the Internet.

Keys to Success

Sell advertising. This is another business that requires face-to-face contact. To be successful, you have to guarantee to distribute a sufficient number of copies of the directory to make it worthwhile for an advertiser to pay you.

Resources

Examples of niche yellow pages:
The Women's Yellow Pages of Philadelphia
http://www.philawyp.com/aboutpages/aboutpages_main.htm
P.O. Box 1002 - Havertown, PA 19083

Directory targeting teachers
http://www.joycevalenza.com/print.html

Ten Top Tips for Success

#1. Specialize

Pick one business, get really good at it and market it constantly. It's easier to succeed if you narrow your market. For instance, sell embroidery services to horse owners and trainers. You learn what that market wants and develop the products that sell. Best of all, the customer base is like a small town where good word of mouth spreads rapidly and brings you many customers.

The worst thing to do is to try to work two or three different businesses at once. Would you entrust your money or your beloved pet to someone who does some pet sitting, sells MLM products, breeds fish and builds carrying cases for birds? No one will understand what business you really have and you won't understand how to reach your market.

#2. Keep current and accurate records

It's easy to think you'll remember, or you'll write it down later. Don't risk your business or incur tax liabilities because you can't verify a business expense or prove that you sold or shipped a product.

#3. Keep overhead low

Resist the urge to buy expensive office equipment and supplies. Use what you have or purchase used or sale items at the cheapest office supply store you can find. Don't buy all the "get rich quick" programs you'll find on the Internet. Take advantage of your library and the government agencies that offer enormous quantities of free information. Get free counseling from SCORE

Ten Top Tips for Success

available through the Small Business Administration. Do use a good quality business card and other marketing materials, however. The rule of thumb is if it can't help you make money, spend as little as possible on it.

#4. Pay your bills on time

If you need to buy from distributors or wholesalers for your business, pay your bills on time. If you develop a good relationship with your suppliers, they will be more likely to let you delay or reduce payments if you run into trouble later on. You never know what diaster—hurricane, earthquake, major illness—could befall you and your business.

Good relationships with vendors is another way to ensure good word of mouth within your business community. It also ensures you get priority service from them when you need it to satisfy your own customers.

#5. Continue your education

Regardless of which business you choose, there is more you can learn about it. If you're performing a trade or craft, take classes to sharpen your skills. If you're already a subject matter expert, take classes in accounting or marketing. Experts also command higher fees than generalists.

#6. Be discreet about your customers

Never discuss what you're doing for a customer in public with friends or acquaintances. Don't share your feelings about a customer, especially the difficult ones, in public. There is no telling who might overhear. You could seriously damage your business if you became known as a gossip or blabbermouth.

#7. Market your service or product continually

Never stop looking for customers. Many small businesses have been devastated because they relied on one large customer who suddenly ended their business relationship. Keep your name in front of your potential customer base. Once you have some experience and a customer base, team with another related but non-competing business and jointly market your products or services. This expands the potential customer base for you both (or more).

#8. Set your standards high

Consistently provide first class service in everything you do. Please note the "consistently." You will not succeed if you only do good work when you're interested in the project or you like the customer. Be a professional and perform every job as though your mortgage payments depended on it.

#9. Be prepared to handle emergencies

If you work with live animals, know where the nearest 24-hour animal hospital or veterinary office is located and how you would pay for their services. If you rely on a vehicle for your business, have a back-up plan if the battery in your SUV is dead one winter morning.

If you're a sole proprietor, develop a standing arrangement with a trusted friend, family member or colleague to handle your business in the event you suddenly became unavailable or incapacitated. There's no excuse not to have a back-up plan for the typical disasters that can happen in any business.

#10. Final and most important tip—Keep Your Priorities Straight

Family first, business second. Never sacrifice your family, your health or your ethics for your business. It's easy to get consumed with your business, especially one you truly enjoy operating. When the business gets in the way of family, health or morality, change the business. Your life is more important.

OK, now get started and make lots of money!

syn keyword GoodWord transparent your

101 Home based Businesses for Pet Lovers

Index

a

accounting programs
  MYOB   *14, 15*
  Quicken   *14, 15*
  Simply Accounting   *14, 15*
advertising specialties   *43*
Advertising Specialty Institute, The   *45*
Alpaca Registry Inc., The   *316*
alpacas
  raising   *315*
American Bee Journal   *77*
American Beekeeping Federation   *74, 75, 77*
American Birding Assn.   *81, 83*
American Boarding Kennels Assn.   *144*
American Farriers Organization   *86*
American Hairless Terrier   *140*
American Horse Publications (AHP)   *178*
American Kennel Club   *139, 146, 146, 176, 177, 284*
  breed rescue   *182*
  microchip registry   *292*
  referral search   *295, 296*
  Registered Handlers Program   *148*
American Pet Products Manufacturers Assn. (APPMA)   *39, 40, 132, 198, 247, 354, 356*
American Red Cross   *36*
  Pet First Aid   *36, 102*
American Riding Instructors Assn. (ARIA)   *173, 175*
animal actors   *46*
Animal Behavior Society   *52*
animal behavior therapist   *50*
animal massage therapist   *53*
Animal Planet   *47, 49*
animals, custom stuffed   *130*
animal sounds cd-rom   *56*
ant colony   *59*
aquarium maintenance   *62*
Aquarium Professionals Group   *89*
aromatherapist   *64*
art broker   *67*
Athan, Mattie Sue   *80*
Audubon Society
  local   *79, 81, 106*
  National   *83*

b

Backer, H.H. Associates Inc.   *37*
BASSCO Inc. (advertising specialties)   *43, 45*
Beauchamp, Richard G.   *141*
bed and breakfast   *70*
beekeeper   *74*
Benjamin, Carol Lea   *151*
bird day care   *78*
birding guides   *81*
birds
  birding guides   *81*
  cleaning cages of   *106*
  day care   *78*
  raising   *319*
Blacksmith's Journal   *86*
blacksmith or farrier   *84*
book marks   *223*
Brabec, Barbara   *10*
breed fish   *87*
Breeding Dogs For Dummies   *141*
brochures   *17*

build designer dog houses   90
build macquariums   94
business cards, rolodex   20

c
calendar, marketing   21
calendars, custom   122
Canine Cab   304
canine rehabilitation   97
car signs   20
cat breeder   101
cat day care   104
cats
  breeding   101
  catnip, organic   246
  day care   104
  kitty litter delivery   133
Cat Writer's Association, Inc.   178
CD-ROM   56, 56, 56, 57, 57, 123, 345, 345, 346, 364
  calendars   123
  labels   57
checking account, business   12
cleaning bird cages   106
computer pet   109
coupons   16, 25, 287, 309, 352
create paint-by-numbers coloring book   112
critter products   115
critters, products for   115
cross stitch patterns   119
custom calendars   122
custom pet portraits   125
custom screen savers   128
custom stuffed animals   130

d
deliver kitty litter   133
designer jewelry for pet and owner   135
Dibra, Bash   49
dog cross-breeder   138
dog day care   142
Dog Handlers Guild   148
dogs
  Border Collie   179
  canine rehabilitation   97
  cross-breeding   138
  day care   142
  doggy doors   201
  houses, designer   90
  show handler   145
  trainer, electronic   158
  training   149
  walker   152
dog show handler   145
dog trainer   149
dog walker   152
dvds for pets   155

e
Eckstein, Warren   52
electronic dog trainer   158
embroidery   161
exotic pets, showing   338
export consultant   165

f
farrier   84
ferret
  see also *Modern Ferret*   341
fish
  aqaurium mainenance   62
  aquarium, fishless   169

376

aquariums, ecologically correct   207
breeding   87
Koi Ponds   334
Macquariums   94
fishless aquarium   169
Fiumara, Georgianne   222
flyers   19
freelance riding instructor   173
freelance writer   176

g
geese patrol   179
Grosjean, Nelly   66
grow worms   183
guarantees   26, 26, 51, 54, 88, 102, 150, 159, 212, 253, 270, 272, 295, 336, 369
guardianship   34
Guide to a Well-Behaved Parrot   80

h
Haggerty, Arthur J.   49
Hammond, Lee   127
Handmade for Profit   132
Hoffman Publications   86
Homemade Money   10
homeowners associations   29
Hopkins, Tom   200
horse boarding   186
horse cargo trailer service   190
horses
  blacksmith or farrier   84
  boarding   186
  cargo trailer service   190
  guide   305
How to Draw Lifelike Portraits

from Photographs   127
How to Get Your Pet into Show Business   49
How To Open and Operate a Bed & Breakfast   73
How to Start a Home Based Mail Order Business   222
How to Start & Operate a Mail Order Business   222

i
importer   192
incorporate business   12, 14, 31, 242, 254
independent sales agent   197
install doggy doors   201
insurance   20, 30, 31, 51, 70, 79, 98, 101, 104, 106, 133, 142, 149, 153, 187, 190, 202, 236, 237, 242, 248, 254, 264, 270, 271
Internal Revenue Service   10, 73
international pet travel   203

j
Jewelry Making for Fun and Profit   137
jewelry, designer   135

k
Kaesar and Blair   43
Kamoroff, Bernard   15
keepsake pillows   231
kits   22

l
lawsuits   30, 32, 34
lease ecologically correct aquariums   207

377

list or sell pet businesses   *211*
LLC   *14, 31*
local portal website   *215*

m

Madden, Denise   *52*
magnets   *20, 43*
mail order supplies   *219*
make book marks   *223*
make electronic photo albums   *227*
make keepsake pillows   *231*
Memoirs of a Pet Therapist   *52*
mobile pet grooming   *235*
Modern Ferret   *341, 343, 344, 361*
Musante, Linda   *137*
MYOB (program)   *14*

n

National Animal Interest Alliance   *35*
National Audubon Society   *83*
National Craft Association (NCA)   *121, 132, 226, 234*
National Mail Order Assn.   *222*
Nerius, Maria Given   *137*

o

online dating service   *238*
operate a pet retirement home   *242*
organic catnip products   *246*
ownership   *34*

p

paint-by-numbers coloring book   *112*
paw casts   *248*

Pet Age   *37*
Pet Business   *37*
Pet Product News   *37, 354*
PETA   *35*
pet astrologer   *251*
pet bakery   *254*
pet carpentry   *257*
pet carry all   *260*
pet cemetery   *263*
pet club of the month   *266*
pet detective   *269*
pet food delivery   *271*
pet gift baskets   *274*
pet humor website   *278*
Pet Industry Distributors Assn. (PIDA)   *39, 40*
Pet Industry Joint Advisory Council (PIJAC)   *39*
pet insurance   *281*
pet party planner   *285*
pet photographer   *287*
pet referral service   *294*
pet registration   *290*
Pet Sitters International   *79, 154, 297, 299*
pet sitting   *297*
pet stationery   *300*
pet taxi   *303*
photo albums, electonic   *227*
pillows, keepsake   *231*
portraits, custom pet   *125*
postcards   *20, 296*
price   *22*
Professional Handlers Assn.   *148*
Professional Mobile Groomers Intl.   *237*
promomart.com/   *45*
Promotional Products Association

378

International (PPAI)   45
publish horse friendly guide   305
publish local pet newspaper   308
puzzle maker   311

q
Quicken(program)   14

r
raise alpacas   315
raise birds   319
raise crickets   323
reminder service   326

s
search engine placement software   17
Selling for Dummies   200
sell invisible fencing   330
sell mobile bird cages   332
set up koi ponds   334
show exotic pets   338
Silliphant, Leight and Sureleigh   200
Simon, Julian L.   222
Simply Acounting(program)   14
Small Time Operator   15
Standard Rate and Data Services (SRDS)   38
Stankus, Jan   73
Star Pet: How to Make Your Pet a Star   49

start niche magazine   341
stock photos and drawings   345
summer camp for dogs   348

t
tour operator   351
trade shows   40, 136, 162, 262, 355, 355, 356

u
Uncle Milton Ind.   59, 59, 61, 61
Universal Product Code UPC   58
upscale pet products   354

v
Veterinary Aromatherapy   66
video or dvd producer   357
virtual cemetery and memorial center   360

w
word of mouth   22
worms, growing   183
write a guide for would-be breeders   363
writer, freelance   176

y
yellow pages directory   367

z
zoning   29, 51

Are you considering a small dog for your household but aren't sure which is the right one for you?

Visit us at http://www.toybreeds.com for honest information—what's good and what's bad—about all the Toy breeds recognized by the American Kennel Club (AKC).

We'll help match you to the best small dog for your lifestyle.

Once you identify the breed(s) you're considering, get one of our Special Reports on your breed of choice. Each report of approximately 30-pages is available for immediate download and filled with no-nonsense information on:

▷ How to select a healthy, good-tempered puppy

▷ What the common health problems of the breed are

▷ How much grooming and maintenance he'll need

▷ Where you should buy your puppy

▷ What protections you get from puppy lemon laws

▷ Why animal shelters are NOT a good place to get a dog

▷ and much more

You get all this information and more!

100% Satisfaction Guaranteed.
Sales price refunded if not satisfied.

Visit us at http://www.toybreeds.com/specialreports.htm

Order Form
send check or money order to:
toybreeds.com
1198 Pacific Coast Highway D-129
Seal Beach, CA 90740

Qty	Title	Price[*]
	101 Home Businesses for Pet Lovers in paperback	$19.95 5.00 Shipping[*] $24.95
	101 Home Businesses for Pet Lovers on CDROM only	$12.95 4.00 Shipping[*] $16.95
	How to Start a Pet Sitting Business *(and what to do once you have)* Three-ring binder with CD-ROM of forms	$24.95 8.50 Shipping[*] $33.45
	How to Start a Pet Sitting Business *(and what to do once you have)* CD-ROM version including forms	$14.95 4.00 Shipping[*] $18.95

Ship to:

Name _____

Address _____

City _____ State _____ Zip _____

[*]Shipping price for continental U.S. only. Email us for Hawaii, Alaska and international rates.